LEADERSHIP
TRAINING
THROUGH GAMING

LEADERSHIP TRAINING
THROUGH GAMING

Power, People and Problem-solving

Elizabeth M Christopher and Larry E Smith

**Kogan Page, London/Nichols Publishing
Company, New York**

First published in Great Britain in 1987
by Kogan Page Ltd,
120 Pentonville Road, London N1 9JN

Reprinted 1988
Reprinted 1989
Reprinted 1990

British Library Cataloguing in Publication Data

Christopher, Elizabeth M.
  Leadership training through gaming.
  1. Management games
  I. Title   II. Smith, Larry E.
  658.4'0353   HD30.26

  ISBN 1-85091-313-7

First published in the USA in 1987
by Nichols Publishing Company
PO Box 96, New York, NY 10024

Library of Congress Cataloging in Publication Data

Christopher, Elizabeth M.
  Leadership training through gaming.

  Bibliography: p.
  1. Leadership—Simulation methods.   2. Management
games.   3. Management—Simulation methods.   I. Smith,
Larry E.   II. Title.
HD57.7.C53   1987   658.4'07353   87-12362
ISBN 0-89397-284-3

Printed and bound in Great Britain by
Biddles Ltd, Guildford and King's Lynn

Contents

Foreword

This book has been written for anybody who wants to play games in settings where they are formally responsible for leadership training with groups of people. This applies not only to professionals such as teachers, social workers, youth leaders, cross-cultural communication experts, human resources development consultants and health professionals, but also to those not formally trained but equally professional, such as community leaders.

What follows was written with this very wide diversity of potential game leaders in mind. We apologize if it seems like a statement of the obvious to some readers.

The teaching profession is full of dire warnings about the 'dangers' of using games and simulations as learning strategies because of their capacity to arouse strong emotions in the players. It is true that games evoke delight and anger, as anybody knows who has played 'Snakes and Ladders' with young children, or watched a football match. There is no denying that teachers who use games, role-plays, and simulations in the classroom are taking a risk with their own and their participants' confidence and self-esteem.

Those of us who are prepared to take this risk do so as a calculated gamble, because the pay-off seems to be so high in terms of active involvement of students in the process of their own learning. Furthermore, we think the argument that serious games are dangerous is often both overstated and one-sided. We believe that games are harmless enough in themselves; the explosive elements — both constructive and destructive — come from the ways in which they are presented, directed, and debriefed by the game leader. Teachers are well aware of this, which is why some of them prefer to avoid the whole experience. We have adopted a different policy, by describing in this book, as fully as we can, where we think game leaders might encounter problems, how to avoid them if possible, and how to defuse them if they do occur. We hope readers will enjoy the book as well as find it useful. We welcome and wish every success to 'new recruits' in gaming, and we salute those who, like ourselves are 'old hands'.

Acknowledgements

We would like to thank the following people for the help they gave us, directly and/or indirectly, in preparing this book:

Erica Bates, Allan Bordow, and Oliver Fiala, University of New South Wales, Sydney, for their contribution to the development of many of the ideas in this book, and to Erica Bates in particular for sharing her debriefing skills.

Mary Bitterman, Director of the Institute of Culture and Communication, East-West Center, Honolulu, for the help the Institute gave us in preparing the manuscript.

Fred Goodman, School of Education, University of Michigan, Ann Arbor, for his original game "Gerontology", reproduced with his permission in Barry Moore, *Australian Management Games*, 1978, Sydney: UNSW Press.

Anne Gorman, Managing Director, Social Impacts, Pty Ltd, Sydney, for her cooperation during the final revisions.

Joyce Gruhn and her colleagues in the Institute of Culture and Communication, East-West Center, for their hard work and personal involvement in preparing the final draft for publication.

Elizabeth Leigh, President of ADSEGA (The Australian Decision/ Simulation and Educational Gaming Association), care of 19 Ryries Parade, Cremorne, NSW 2090, Australia, for her unfailing help with game material.

The participants from the Japan-America Institute of Management Science, Honolulu, who pilot-tested many of the games.

The participants of the 1984 Workshop on Cross-Cultural Understanding, Language Institute of Japan, Odawara, for their cooperation in testing several of our cross-cultural games.

B W Neville and R S Hubbard, members of ADSEGA, from whose game 'The Multi-Purpose, Multi-Phasic, Tower Building Blocks Game' we adapted 'Infernal Towers'.

Maureen O'Brien, East-West Center, for her editing.

Eileen Quigley and Narelle Isaacs, formerly of the School of Health Administration, University of New South Wales, from whose original idea we developed the simulation game 'New Year's Eve Hat'.

Richard Via, Institute of Culture and Communication, East-West Center, for his incomparable insights on simulations.

Introduction: Why and How to Play Games

Experienced game leaders will not be surprised by the following story. A colleague of ours was newly appointed as training officer of a large corporation. Keen to impress, she suggested to the managing director (MD) that she use a games programme to teach a proposed leadership skills seminar for senior managers. From behind his big desk, the MD looked at her coldly over his spectacles and replied: 'My managers aren't here to play games!'

His retort was a practical example of what Eric Berne (1964) calls game-playing in real life. The MD was demonstrating to the newcomer that he, not she, was in control of his company's training programmes — hence the 'I win, you lose' put-down. However, he was also expressing a commonly held belief that games for learning are a waste of time and money, because companies pay for their staff to attend training programmes which offer to improve their productivity, not entertain them.

What the MD was not taking into account was the fact that professional productivity depends on more than a trained capacity to absorb information, facts and figures. Learning and problem-solving are part of a continual and lifelong process of change in attitudes, values and beliefs which occurs through a never-ending negotiation between new information and what they already 'know'. Games, role-plays and simulations provide a kind of 'base camp' from which to make forays into new worlds. Games are known territory; their parameters are set. They have roles and rules, beginnings, endings, and limited consequences. They are comfortable learning grounds and good to have in training programmes because the process of exploration into a new world is not without pain.

Games support and foster the emotional component that all learning contains — even learning something as abstract as 'two and two make four'. The personality of the teacher, the teaching method (with its respective emphasis on cognitive, emotional or skills learning) and the individual learning styles of the students will appreciably affect the extent to which they become involved with the process of mathematics. For example, some people will recognize the basic principles of mathematics more quickly and effectively by a primarily cognitive teaching method such as a 'chalk and talk', because they like facts to be presented to them in linear and orderly arguments whose logic they approve of and understand. Others —like a friend of ours — may not be so happy with this kind of teaching strategy because they need to be able to relate abstractions to experience.

Our friend spent years bewailing the fact that she was 'not good at maths' until finally we pointed out she had no problems, as far as we could see, in balancing her cheque book, working out the interest rates on her mortgage, comparing two unequally sized jars of coffee in the supermarket to find the cheaper, and calculating how long it would take her to drive to San Francisco in her battered old Ford if she stopped for afternoon tea with Aunt Jessica in Fresno.

'But none of that is mathematics!' cried our friend: 'That's just *life!*' So it is, and so some people will learn more about mathematics through experience-based teaching methods like games and simulations rather than hearing lectures or reading books. Admittedly there are published taxonomies which argue that some types of learning are not emotional, but our experience over two lifetimes of teaching is that it is impossible even to begin to control the learning processes of ourselves and others unless there is prior recognition of the emotional — or feelings — components involved.

Arguably, these feelings can be grouped under three headings:

(1) The desire to keep some kind of *control* — to have *power* — over situations, oneself and other people, as they shift and change through the vicissitudes of life.
(2) The need continually to adjust one's *personal relationships* to keep pace with the changes.
(3) The *intellectual challenge* of solving problems as they occur along the way.

In other words, learning — which we equate with problem-solving and define as relevant change within the learner — can be said to be about *power*, *people* and *problem-solving*: and so can games, which is why they can be constructed as such effective learning tools. Anybody who has ever played any game — tag or tennis, cards or charades, snakes and ladders or snooker, pass-the-parcel or pool, football, basketball or backgammon — will recognize the same motivations in all of them: the desire to win (which includes the pleasure of beating one's opponents); the impulse to support one's partners or team-mates; and the challenge, born of a kind of problem-solving curiosity, to see the game through and find out 'what happens at the end'.

People experience these emotions in different degrees and proportions. Some enjoy the sociability of a game more than the desire to win, others will cheat, if need be, to beat the other players. Some play games to keep fit — which is a form of control over self; others prefer the excercise of huddling immobile over pieces on a chessboard, pondering the problem of moving towards checkmate. Yet most games are likely to evoke the whole range of power-feelings, people-feelings and problem-solving, or goal-oriented, feelings; which is why virtually everybody likes games in some form or other.

How does all this relate to leadership training through gaming? Like learning, leadership is concerned with power, people and goals. Leadership means acquiring followers; that is, persuading people to do what their leaders want done, preferably while being grateful to those same leaders for giving them the opportunity to do it — and simultaneously encouraging them to acquire new skills and expertise to set their own goals for accomplishment of the tasks their leaders set them. Leadership also means coaching people to accept responsibility for their own actions, so that leaders can delegate more and more to their followers while they themselves 'walk purposefully down the corridors of power'.

Playing games can teach potential leaders — including, of course, game leaders themselves — how to do all these things, by demonstrating the cause-and-effect relationship between leader-behaviour, follower-response, and task accomplishment. No doubt some charismatic leaders are born, not made, and nobody need teach such people anything about uses of power; but it is our contention that most of us who want, or who are required, to become leaders need to be taught a basic set of skills.

In our experience of organizational behaviour in high-tech societies, employees arrive at leadership by relatively narrow and specialized paths. They may start as accountants, computer programmers, social workers, systems analysts, teachers, technical sales staff, nurses or whatever. If they do well in their chosen fields, sooner or later they are promoted to management level; and management usually implies the need for leadership.

Not all leaders are managers and managers do not necessarily have to be leaders (they may be managing a set of accounts, for example). Nevertheless, new managers often have to acquire a range of interpersonal skills which they may seldom have needed before, and which previously they may even have avoided, such as the use of power, the handling of conflict, small group negotiation, and the assessment of followers' responses and performances according to criteria defined by specific objectives. Moreover, in today's global village, many organizational leaders may now find themselves operating in multicultural contexts where English is an international language and leader behaviour has to accommodate itself to many cultural differences.

Leaders — and remember that this also means game leaders — have to maintain an effective balance among power, people's feelings, and the need to solve problems, meet deadlines, and achieve objectives. It may be that some individuals' leadership styles become unbalanced through the demands of their personalities, professional backgrounds, and other psychological or logistical factors. For example, leaders who are temperamentally 'turned on' by the action of working through a problem towards a solution may choose to participate rather than lead — even when delegation would probably encourage more maturity and motivation in their followers. Thus some game directors find it difficult or impossible to leave the players free to get on with the game, even when it is in the players' best interests that they should do so.

Other leaders may become so personally involved with their team that they overlook members' lack of relevant skills. Game leaders do this when they plunge their players into emotional experiences they are not equipped to handle; or leaders may be so task-minded that they issue instructions and expect performances without attempting to keep players' morale and motivation high. Others may have such a strong need for power that they dominate a debriefing session, even when the players know more than the leader about the real-life circumstances to which the game results might apply.

Organizational examples also illustrate the argument that leader-style biases materially affect followers' behaviour. Let us suppose, for instance, that the office photocopier breaks down on a very busy day, that nobody on the staff seems to know what to do about it, and that there is urgent work to be finished. The office manager is an action-minded woman who used to operate the machine constantly and grew accustomed to its breakdowns before she was elevated to a higher status, where now she has her copying done for her by subordinates. In this situation, she sighs, puts aside her essential work (like next year's budget), goes into the photocopy room, and fixes the machine.

Presumably she decided, on the basis of experience, that this was the quickest way to restart production in the circumstances, and she may have been right. However, her action may not have been the most effective in terms of leadership. Why was nobody else trained to repair minor malfunctions in the copier? Why did the copier keep breaking down? Why were the staff not motivated sufficiently to find some way of solving the problem without having to take the manager away from her work? The answers relate to seven kinds of power that leaders have at their disposal (Hersey and Blanchard, 1977).

She could have delegated her *expertise*, rather than using it herself, to instruct her subordinates how to fix small breakdowns, now and in the future. She might have *information* about a local printer who could be relied on in emergencies. She might think about raising office morale by using her *useful connections* with senior management (or by being married to Mr Xerox) to provide a brand new copier. She might also *demand* that the person who last used the machine should in the future be responsible for its repair. She might use her *personality* to persuade the staff to commit themselves to the responsibility of keeping the office running smoothly at all times. On the other hand, she may decide that most staff members are not yet ready for this kind of responsibility. Then she would use her *legitimate authority* as office manager to lock the copyroom door and *reward* a few carefully selected subordinates by entrusting them with the secret of the key's hiding place.

Effective leaders have acquired knowledge and self-knowledge to use these seven sources of power appropriately, depending on the capabilities, receptivity and responsiveness of their followers and the nature of the task. But how are inexperienced leaders to know what is appropriate behaviour for them, and when and why such behaviour should occur? This is where games are so useful. Games make participants' leadership behaviour — including that of the game director — both visible and audible, in constructed contexts that are both magnifications and simplifications of real-life situations and events. They serve to illustrate individuals' relationships to organizational, social, natural and mechanical structures in terms of power, human relationships and problem-solving.

Virtually all the participants — from many cultural backgrounds — who have played our games in the United States, Australia, and Japan have reported that as a result they have gained insights not only into behaving as leaders but also into the behaviour patterns of colleagues, including those of foreigners. Admittedly, there are other ways besides games to learn about leadership but nothing else, in our experience, evokes that flash of recognition, like a gasp of the breath — sometimes literally so — when a leadership tactic is seen dramatically to fail or succeed in game form.

Unfortunately, this flash of recognition does not happen automatically every time a learning game is played, and there is virtually no solid theory to explain why games can be such effective learning strategies in some circumstances and not in others. We think the key lies in game directors' leadership powers and their relationship to their players; and that they are likely to use games more successfully for their teaching needs if they acquire more understanding of how to present, direct and debrief games in ways that suit both their individual leadership styles and the motivational needs of their followers.

One important example is that some players seem to become more motivated to learn if they are allowed to take *observer* rather than *participant* roles; yet much of the literature of simulation games suggests that all learners need to participate, not merely to observe a game, if they are to learn anything from it. This assumes that observers are not participants. We take the position that they are, and that people will learn a great deal about the assumptions, dynamics and hidden meanings within a given game situation by watching it.

In gaming, observers see the game as a whole, and therefore derive more objective meanings than those that the players derive. This is because the players interpret the activity according to a narrower, more personal experience. Unfortunately, learning games are usually directed so that the only observers, as such, are those leading the game. Thus the leader is frequently the only person to see the participants' actions in overview and therefore the only one capable of perceiving how the pattern of conflict or consensus has evolved. The group is dependent on one person's views (ie the group leader), unmodified by perhaps completely different impressions that others may have received while participating in the game.

Leadership is about increasing the motivation and maturity of followers. Therefore, everything game leaders do with players should work towards leading them in the direction of overcoming their passivity and developing responsibility for their own learning. So why not sometimes use games in which only a few people are active players while the rest function as an audience? Or videotape the game and play it back afterwards so that the 'actors' become the 'audience' and everyone can see the game-pattern of behaviour without being totally dependent on their leader to tell them what happened?

The concept that games create a pattern, or structure, of action is essential to understanding how they function as learning strategies. It is the business of the game leader to ensure — by a number of means — that the players examine this structure for themselves and understand how the process of cause-and-effect has built itself up out of the relationship between game leader and player-followers, and between the players themselves. Players cannot always stand back, so to speak, and watch this process in overview while it is happening, even though some people by temperament are more objective than others. Nor can game directors themselves always be aware of the nature, extent and effect of their behaviour on the group unless they constantly seek feedback from the group.

Thus the game situation is set up in the first place by the director with specific objectives in mind. It is the director, not the players, who first 'sets the scene' and continues to monitor the action — behaviour which, to a critical extent, will affect the players' activity. Different kinds of action, and different 'plots' will be created,

depending on the game director's leadership style. This statement
will appear simplistic if it is taken to mean no more than that the
action of a simulation game will differ with every director and every
group of players, but the implications are more profound than this.

It may be that Carl Rogers' (1969) word 'facilitator' for team
leader is misleading to describe those who direct simulations, classroom role-plays, and games. The term 'facilitator' is intended to convey the notion that the game director is non-participant in the sense
of refraining from influencing the outcome. The opposite, however,
is more likely to be true because, where games are concerned, the
non-participating organizer is perceived by the players to be in the
position of final authority. This suggests that game directors must
not abrogate but *interpret* the leader roles that players have ascribed
to them by consenting to play the game.

Emotions in gaming are always likely to run high — like those of
the player who told us, three years after the event: 'I was angry, and
I'm *still* angry at what happened to me in the game!' Fortunately,
her anger was a constructive emotion that fuelled her energy to work
for the rehabilitation of handicapped people — which was what the
game was about. The game is called 'New Year's Eve Hat', and you
will find it in Chapter Six. Failure on the part of game leaders to
recognize the nature of players' responses can lead to resentment,
hostility and rejection both of leader and game results. Leaders will
become confused and distressed, especially if they have been told by
other educators that the game in question is 'a good one' — or, even
worse, 'fail-safe'!

Hazards like these, which educators acknowledge about the use of
games as teaching tools, deter some trainers and teachers from
employing them at all. Nevertheless, games have enormous potential
and they may have more power in some cases than any other teaching
method. Working with a team to achieve its leader's and members'
potential through gaming is a truly creative task. It can be compared
to the job of a theatre director, who guides actors to interpret their
roles in the process of improvising or staging a play. This does not
mean that game leaders should coach players how to 'act'. Instead
they should help them to call on their natural emotions so that they
behave as they feel they would do if the situation were not a game
but real life. In effect, they tell the players: 'Find out how you
behave in this situation. Was your response as effective as you would
wish it to be? If not, these are some of the ways you might like to
consider changing it in real life.'

Like all leaders, game and theatre directors have to work with a
collection of individuals and turn them into an ensemble whose
united efforts will be greater than the sum of its parts. Therefore,
the leader must learn to recognize how much responsibility each

individual team member is capable of assuming at any given point and what that person's greatest contribution to the team is likely to be. Theatre directors, when they have selected a play or a theme for improvisation, impose more or less direction on the actors depending on who they are. For example, with a cast of professionals who have worked together frequently, there may be no need to be authoritarian, unless there are in-group dissensions; with a group of amateurs, on the other hand, or with professional actors who have never worked together before, the director may need to oversee closely the allocation of roles, and may have to provide a great deal of explanation.

This is leadership behaviour which Hersey and Blanchard (1977) call 'high in task and low in relationship', but the proportion will vary depending on the mix of actors. The director continues to give explanations or lead discussions until the actors gain a sufficiently clear understanding of what they need and want to do. The director then initiates the dramatic action as the individual actors start the process of becoming an ensemble or a team. Their leader is still highly task-oriented but now there is more room for human feelings and relationships to develop as the actors explore the dimensions of their roles: now the director focuses less on the task as a whole and more on the encouragement and support of individual actors in scenes where they appear to lack confidence or skill. Finally, the director delegates the entire task of interpreting the drama to the cast and — if there is to be a public performance — sits in the back row on the first night, applauds loudly, and rushes backstage afterwards to tell everybody how wonderful they are.

How does this sequence of behaviour compare with your own, assuming that you intend to use a particular game to demonstrate something for a group of learners?

(1) You decide in advance why you want this game for this group. If you have had no contact with them at this point, the decision rests entirely with you. The more you know about them, directly or by report, the more likely you will be to select an appropriate game — but the risk element is still fairly high. We have asked senior managers many times to play simple games with building blocks that would appear more suitable for children, but we usually introduce the games with a short, serious explanation about what we are trying to achieve, in order to lessen the chances of their rejecting the whole idea.

(2) Take as much time as you need to explain the game to the players and ask questions to ensure the rules and roles are understood. Give the role-takers any guidelines they need for action within the game's represented setting.

- The only relationship that you *must* have with your players to start with is that these busy and often self-important people should perceive you to be a credible and trustworthy person from whom they are likely to learn something to their advantage. It would be nice if you could present yourself as being likeable as well, but do not worry too much about that now. It is more important at this stage that they respect you rather than like you.

- You have to be task-minded and reasonably power-oriented, or your more theoretical and more aggressive team-members — not to mention the non-motivated and non-assertive ones — will keep you talking forever rather than getting on with the game, or may even be on the brink of rejecting the whole idea. You have to give them plenty of information in a confident manner in order to keep them with you until they get involved in the game. In other words, at this point, your wisest assumption — unless you know definitely to the contrary — is that your team is low in motivation, unsure of what is going to happen next, and very likely suffering from feelings of inadequacy. Therefore, you need to project a strong, confident image — which does not mean an aggressive one — and convey the reassuring impression that you have played this game lots of times before and it is a winner.

- Remember the seven sources of power you have at your disposal — to be used sparingly or laid on with a trowel, before the game, during it, and at any time you may need them during its debriefing. In short, sell **yourself**!

(i) Your *expertise* should have preceded you. **Project your expertise!** Players should know in advance that you will be in charge of their group for this session. If the group is obstreperous, do not hesitate to remind them of your expertise. Tell anecdotes about your previous experiences of playing games, for example, and show by your manner and bearing that you are in authority.

(ii) You may need the power of *important connections*. **Project your connections!** Depending on the circumstances and the group, it may ease your path if the most senior member of the firm has introduced you — or if you can mention having run a training session with the Prime Minister.

(iii) You have *information* power. **Project your knowledge!** You can tell people where they can learn more about whatever it is they want to know; you can answer their questions and share your insights borne of experience.

(iv) You have the power of your *personality*, which you have spent years practising to make your most powerful teaching skill. **Project your personality!** For example, you may have acquired a kind of calm authority which conveys the message: 'I know what I'm talking about; you will learn something of value by listening to me!' Some personalities have this attribute to such an extent that they become 'gurus' to thousands, perhaps millions, of people. Or you may be an older teacher who has learned to rely on your feelings, and your authority may be derived from the vulnerable and gentle wisdom of the years. Or perhaps you command respect by the power of your mind to grasp and retain a wide range of detailed information. On the other hand, you may rely on your ability to charm and delight your students: by the way you wear your clothes, dress your hair, and gesture with your hands, you may offer yourself as a model and your students may find themselves thinking 'I want to be like that!' Or you may be able to build a rapport with students through your sensitivity to their feedback, verbal and non-verbal; and may have developed a highly flexible teaching style that can accommodate itself to many kinds of learning. Or you may be so knowledgeable, have such a powerful recall of facts and figures, that you command respect.

(v) You have the power of your *position*. **Project your status!** You have been specially invited here to lead this group. The whole situation is set up to communicate the message that you are in charge.

(vi) You have the power to *reward*. **Project your 'kindly' image!** Rewards come in many shapes and sizes; they can be a friendly smile, a word of congratulation, the making of a little ritual of handing over the money to the winner. Above all, you have the power to make the game a rewarding experience for at least most of the players.

(vii) You have the power to *punish*. **Project your authority!** This power may be very limited. If your players are powerful people themselves, they are not going to burst into tears at your frown; nevertheless, punishment is at your disposal to some extent. A calculated silence, a vigorous shake of the head, a thoughtful stare — one or all of these things can demonstrate this power if you need to use it.

Having digressed to this extent, we now return to our sequence of events.

(3) Players and observers now know what the roles are and understand the rules. With any luck and/or skill on your part they are

becoming interested (if only mildly at this stage) in the action. As the motivation level of the group rises, and as they become more capable of taking responsibility themselves for the game, you allow yourself proportionately more human interaction — more people-oriented behaviour. You supply information and listen to individual problems that may arise as the game gets under way; you generally become more encouraging. However, keep the task firmly in mind, for you cannot yet rely on the situation to take care of itself.

(4) The game is now up and running. You are now an enthusiastic and sympathetic follower of the action, and your only intervention is to throw a problem back to the players when they try to dump it on you. There may be occasions when you *have* to interfere — though we find it difficult to think of one; maybe if younger players start fighting? Basically, however, you are now in the position of the theatre director who watches the final dress rehearsal from the back row of the gallery. The players are deeply engaged in building and/or observing a structure of dramatic action that is theirs, not yours. Your behaviour is neither interactive nor focused on task. You are functioning as a discerning observer of the problem-solving process.

(5) Afterwards in debriefing, you remain in this delegatory posture, allowing the group to take responsibility for its own conclusions, which will be based on direct and indirect experience of the game on the part of the players, and indirect experience on the part of the observers. Then you move in again because you have another task, to help group members relate their conclusions, ideas, concerns — whatever — to their existing knowledge and life experience. You monitor this discussion carefully, alert to correct any mistakes of fact, to add more information, to offer examples and suggestions, and to ask constructive questions in order to enlarge debate and encourage creative problem-solving.

However, you do only what you think is required of you. You are now almost completely out of the power-phase and well into a people-oriented, problem-solving mode, but you must be prepared to pick up power again if the group seems to lack the maturity and responsibility to take control of their own learning. In other words, throughout the whole game experience, you have moved continually between power, people, and the problem to be solved. You have involved yourself with your players in three different kinds of motivation, in sequence and in combination.

The group accorded you the degree of *power* that you needed to accomplish *your* task (which was not necessarily the one they would have chosen for themselves) without intruding too much on their own sense of power. They might have been highly skilled specialists in their own fields, timid novices, or assertive teenagers, but you persuaded them — using your people-skills — to trust you to guide them safely and competently through the exercise. In addition, they have benefited from the stimulus of interaction with each other as partners or opponents within the game scenario. You and they have also been challenged by the *problem* of finding explanations for their game experiences that they can usefully relate to their real worlds.

Relevant theory argues that virtually all human motivation can be grouped into these three categories — to achieve power, to influence people, to solve problems — which makes game-forms remarkably appropriate for learning about leadership. In summary, since the game director is the person ultimately responsible for choosing and running a game, the behaviour of the leader is the key variable which will determine what kind of learning the participants derive from the whole exercise. It is true that in all teaching methods the personality of the teacher is critical, which is why no two teachers are interchangeable, no matter how similar their fields. However, when gaming is the learning strategy, the director's *leadership style* is the vital ingredient.

Game-playing, however, would be impossible without games, so on to the next chapter, which deals with warm-ups and other short 'triggers' to promote enthusiasm for learning.

Chapter 1

Warm-ups and Other Short Games

Educators, community workers and other leaders who enjoy using simulations and games often like to begin teaching sessions with one or two 'warm-up' exercises (also known as ice-breakers). Unfortunately, this sometimes results in participants being asked to do quite straightforward things — like introducing themselves — in complicated, time-consuming and even embarrassing ways.

People may be told to interview each other in pairs, for example, and then introduce their partners to the whole group. Or they may be asked to play guessing games about each other, draw self-portraits, or write some personal information on a label to pin on themselves, then go round the room trying to match their likes/ dislikes/personality traits with those of other people, and so on. The arguments for warm-ups are that they create an atmosphere of relaxed informality, so that people get to know each other while simultaneously gaining self-confidence and trust in each other; and that because such games are fun, they provide stimulus for learning.

We agree that these are desirable aims at some point during a training session — though not necessarily at the very beginning — but we find many warm-ups to be a virtual waste of time at any stage. When we have only a few days or even hours in which to introduce busy people to a whole range of new material, everything that happens in the classroom has to be part of a sequence of learning and every exercise needs to perform a number of linked and related functions. Warm-ups must act as triggers for this process, rather like a starter's gun at a race-track, to overcome that initial inertia we are all familiar with when faced with the prospect of having to think.

An essential skill for trainers in time-management is the ability to recognize when gaming is likely to be the most effective strategy and when some other learning method will probably better serve their purposes. For example, new group members are always interested in who everybody is and what they do; the quickest method of providing this information is to label everybody and hand out some essential information about them all, one copy per person. It seems unnecessary to spend half an hour playing games to get people to learn something which they may very likely forget, when instead they can be supplied with a written record they can read in a few minutes and retain for reference.

This suggestion is particularly relevant when the group possesses good social skills and members start moving around of their own accord, shaking hands and chatting briefly with each other. It is only when people seem tense and ill at ease that a game is likely to be the most economical strategy in terms of getting them group-minded as quickly as possible.

An example of when a game is most useful is in assertiveness training. We used to run sessions regularly for the Australian Institute of Management in Sydney, for mixed groups of business people from different organizations all over Australia, including public and private-sector managers. Many of them had not volunteered for the course but had been advised by their superiors to attend, because they were deemed either to lack assertion or to be too aggressive. In fact, we remember one man who had actually been on the first day of his vacation, skiing in the Snowy Mountains, when he was summoned 450 miles back to Sydney by his head office to attend our seminar — presumably, his boss had only just seen a copy of the AIM catalogue of courses.

Thus we were continually having to deal with two very ill-assorted kinds of people: some of them would glare at us and say loudly, 'Well, I can't understand why I'm on this course. I never thought I lacked assertiveness!' And others would avoid our eyes and mutter in embarrassed tones that, yes, probably, er, well, they weren't always very good at speaking up for themselves at meetings and things. The man who had been skiing was so resentful at being with us that he did not utter a single word the whole of the first day — and at that stage we did not know why, which was rather unnerving.

When, to put it bluntly, you have a collection of potential bullies on the one hand and victims on the other, the business of building a workable group dynamic becomes a very tricky affair. On these occasions we usually begin with a game like 'You Choose', in order to give people a chance to settle down a bit, and to give ourselves the opportunity to identify those players who are likely to try and dominate the group — and us — and those who are going to need a lot of encouragement to open their mouths at all.

If you do decide to play one or more warm-up games, you can do more than teach participants each others' names and get them to feel a bit more friendly towards each other, and you can also video-tape the games. It surprises us that few, if any, training manuals recommend videotaping, yet there is almost no formal classroom where recording facilities are unobtainable. Alternatively, a portable audiocassette recorder can provide participants with a means of hearing themselves 'as others hear them'. Neither video nor audiotape has to be replayed immediately — it can be kept for a more appropriate time, or not used at all — but at least it is there if you want it. You have got something tangible that you can use to help participants improve their presentation skills. During a residential course, participants are often very pleased to have something to look at and discuss in the evenings. We think that training manuals do not normally suggest using a video recording system because of trainers' complaints that it takes too long to set up, replay, and analyse a video recording, and that videotaping defeats the purpose of a warm-up, which is to produce an atmosphere that is relaxed and informal, yet conducive to learning. However, we do not agree with this line of thought. Our experience has been that many teachers do not understand and are nervous of educational hardware such as video; they think that such hardware is more complicated than it really is. Provided the equipment is there to start with, a single camera can be set up and left running. Not only will the camera record a surprising amount of the action, but the players, after the first few minutes, seem to forget its presence.

The following are a number of short games that we have found consistently useful for introducing some of the major concepts and assumptions on which the rest of our learning material is based. Each one of these exercises could be adapted appropriately for the beginning of almost any conference or seminar. Furthermore, it is not mandatory to use them as warm-ups at all; they can be played as games in their own right at any time as 'triggers' to start a new section of your material or to illustrate some point you want to make as you go along. All of these games can be played with groups of about five people upwards to almost any number. The largest group with whom we have played them was approximately 150. More than one exercise can be used with the same group, but we find that the most effective technique with games in general is to use them *sparingly*. Therefore, if we begin a session with a warm-up game, we then revert to another teaching method entirely for a while, such as giving a mini-lecture, asking the group to complete a questionnaire, or initiating some kind of discussion. Playing games one after the other is counter-productive for us. We get better results, and students' interest is more sustained, if teaching methods are varied.

'You Choose'

This lasts a minimum of about an hour and considerably longer if the group is large. If, say, you have more than 50 people, you can expect it to take the whole morning. After you have read about it, you may decide that it is worth the time. Any number can play in virtually any classroom, however rigid the seating plan may be. We usually offer it on the morning of the first day of a new course, or seminar, when it takes us comfortably at least to the first coffee break. It is a good game for spotting potential leaders and followers in the group and for noting leadership behaviour that we can refer to later as examples of theory we might want to discuss. It is one of the best warm-ups we know because the players themselves, as they play the game, illustrate its purpose.

First you give a short explanation — which is an art in itself. You need to sound sufficiently authoritative to impress those of your participants who are 'turned on' by power, and yet you do not want to be so theoretical that the highly people-motivated learners 'tune out'. In addition, you have to reassure the problem-solvers that the exercise does have a point, which will become apparent in due course if they will take it (and you) on trust for a while.

Then you divide everyone into small groups; numbers will depend on how many people there are altogether. There may be only one group, say if there are only five people. In our experience the most difficult circumstance under which to put people into groups is when there is a large number of people (more than 50) and they are sitting in rows in fixed seats. If you are faced with this set-up, but would still like to play 'You Choose', this is how you do it.

Ask every third person in the front row, and in every alternate row after that, to raise their hands. This sounds complicated but is not, as the class has to work it out, not you — which is a game in itself and part of the whole 'warm-up' process. Wait patiently until everyone has stopped counting rows and looking at each other to find out who is the third person. You can offer a helpful remark from time to time if you think the process is getting bogged down. Eventually the designated people will identify themselves and raise their hands. Then ask them to call out their names, and post these on a blackboard or flipchart where everyone can see them.

Announce that these people are group leaders. Ask them to introduce themselves to the person on either side of them, and to the two people directly behind them in the next row, or order to form their groups. There will be some twisting and turning around on chairs, but that does not matter. Thus a number of groups are formed, each of five people. There will probably be one or two people left over on the ends of rows and so on, so you could suggest that any 'spares' can introduce themselves to their nearest leader and join up with that leader's group.

The task for each group is to think of *one* warm-up game for *the whole class* to play in five minutes' time. It must be a game that everyone can play easily in the present circumstances, that stimulates everyone's *creative thinking*, and that lasts no more than five minutes. Post the following criteria somewhere:

(1) Think of/invent a game.
(2) Duration five minutes.
(3) To be played by everyone present in the room.
(4) To begin at (five minutes from time of writing).
(5) To stimulate creative thinking.

Ask if anyone has any questions, and answer them, but do not allow yourself to get dragged into a tedious debate. (Highly power-oriented people or people who are low in motivation to play games will often choose to argue rather than cooperate.)

After five minutes call out the name of each leader in turn and ask for their group's suggestion. If they do not have one, put a dash against their name and move on. Keep the whole thing moving briskly. You may end up with half a dozen suggestions against every name, or with no suggestions at all, or with something in between — it does not matter which. This is a fail-safe game providing you keep your head.

Then ask each leader in turn to tell everyone what happened in their group. What did they talk about? If the room is large and the acoustics bad, you may have to repeat or paraphrase what each person says, so the whole class can hear it. Try to post up a few good quotations in any case, just to ensure that everyone has a similar understanding of what has been said, and you have something to refer back to later. Be sure to obtain the speaker's agreement, in every case, that your paraphrase is what the speaker really intended to say. Accept without comment (except for encouragement) anything the leaders tell you, and allow any interruptions from their group members, provided each group does not take more than its fair share of time, depending on the total number of groups.

When everyone has finished, ask them to contemplate the following questions (without insisting on answers), which you are now posting or have prepared in advance. If the group includes members from different cultures, you should emphasize that there may be cultural differences in the ways people answer these questions (and of course you can substitute your questions for ours if you are not dealing with leadership skills).

(1) *Power:* How did each group leader use (or not use) power to complete the task (ie were any of them observably authoritarian, democratic, or 'hands off'?)?
(2) *Motivation:* Did leaders do or say anything that helped to motivate, support or encourage the group?

(3) *Task:* Was it important to all leaders and groups to accomplish the given task, ie to think of or invent a game? Or did some of the discussions turn into get-to-know-you sessions? If this happened, how did the relevant leaders feel about it?

(4) *Challenge:* Were there any emergent leaders in any of the groups who appeared to challenge the designated leader's authority? How did the followers perceive their leaders? Did they perceive them as being capable? Or did they think they could have done better themselves?

If you want to turn 'You Choose' into a larger and more complex game, at this point ask all group members to rate their respective leaders on a scale of one to five, on the four criteria of power, motivation, task and challenge. Then ask the leaders to average out the scores of all their group members and call out the results, which you post. Then solicit further feedback on why a particular leader 'won' by achieving the highest overall score. Get that leader's followers to give you actual examples of their leader's effective leadership.

If your participants are mostly people like statisticians, they may start making a fuss at this point about the exercise being statistically invalid because the samples were so small. 'What do you expect to prove with only three groups?', we remember a man asking contemptuously. We got out of that one by referring to a number of other occasions where the game had indicated — as on this occasion — that effective leadership occurs through a combination of the style of the leader, the temperaments of the followers, and the nature of the task (remember what we wrote earlier about sometimes having to use information and expertise as power tools?).

If you are directing 'You Choose' for the first time, you might want to remember this incident and avoid the problem yourself by stating in advance that you are using the results merely as illustrations of a number of different leadership styles, without trying to draw hard conclusions. On the other hand, if you should decide to play the game on a number of different occasions — particularly if the groups are varied — you can collate the results, write them up for transferral to transparencies, and use an overhead projector to demonstrate to your next group, for example, that leadership appears to be *situation-specific*, which will take you comfortably to a discussion of Hersey's leadership curve (Hersey and Blanchard, 1977). It is worth remembering that, for some reason we have never quite worked out, game participants are often keen to know how their performance compares to those of other groups. Therefore, this kind of feedback is always well received.

Whether you play the short or the long version, you need to reserve five minutes of 'You Choose' in case the participants really do want to play one of the games that was devised or suggested during the exercise. After all, this was ostensibly the object of the activity and you have to be as good as your word. But by this time it may have dawned on them that the medium was the message — the activity itself was the game it was supposed to create.

The game will also have given you some useful information about the participants that you are going to have to work with for the next hour, day, week, or whatever. You will probably have picked out one or two obvious leaders, and you will probably have a fair idea of the amount of motivating you are going to have to do before you can get on with the teaching job. You will know now whether you have on your hands a bright-eyed, bushy-tailed mob of power-hungry executives who will challenge you every step of the way; or a group of potential followers who will hang on your slightest word; or — more likely — some of both or something in between. For example, did all of the groups come up with a game? Or did none of them? The two extremes of small group behaviour in task-oriented situations where there is a designated leader are high and low productivity. The former is argued to be an attribute of effective leadership and motivated followers (Fiedler and Chemers, 1974). Therefore if none of your groups could come up with a product, you are going to need all of your motivation skills in order to teach leadership to this crowd. You will have to 'sell' you material by force of personality — ie by being a benign autocrat. You will also have to participate a great deal in your learners' learning before you can adopt for any length of time a more 'hands off' approach. On the other hand, if every group in 'You Choose' generated several game suggestions and everybody appeared to be willing, eager, and able to participate, then for the rest of the session you can probably afford less personal involvement and more delegation of goal-setting and decision-making to the group.

Remember also that the total exercise will have been experienced by individuals as more or less comfortable depending on their temperaments. You were probably able to demonstrate, to the satisfaction of most, that one cannot generalize about leader behaviour because it depends so much on circumstances. Some people will accept this happily but some will do so reluctantly or not at all because they are the sort of learner, or problem-solver, who intuitively looks for 'the one right answer', and will become quite annoyed with you if you insist that there is no such animal. So be prepared for controversy even with a highly motivated group of participants.

If you are relatively new to gaming, you may want to make 'You Choose' a little easier for yourself by putting a bit more structure into it in order to give you more control over outcomes. For example, you could provide each group with a length of rope or a ball and ask them to devise a game with it, including a set of rules. This takes some of the pressure off the players because you have supplied more input to their thinking and therefore gained more influence over their decisions. This suggestion also applies to experienced gamers who are faced with unruly or potentially explosive groups.

We remember quite well the experience of running a warm-up session for about 18 drop-out adolescents at a youth and community centre in a disadvantaged suburb of a disadvantaged city. They were too peer-oriented to form sub-groups, and when we asked them to think of a game, they came up with something they called 'Treasure Hunt'. They asked us to give them half an hour, disappeared out of the building, and came back not much later with the strangest assortment of items — including a hairbrush, a pack of cigarettes, a can of soup, a scarf, a screwdriver, and a small potted plant. They solemnly asked us to evaluate these goods, the winning item to be the one we thought the most expensive. They made no attempt to disguise the fact that the whole lot had been shoplifted from neighbourhood stores, and, while we appreciated the trust these young people seemed to repose in us, we learned to keep a tighter check on group members whose imagination was not limited by mundane matters of law and order.

Now for another warm-up, called 'Brainstorm'.

'Brainstorm'

We play this game primarily to generate a lot of ideas quickly, to convey a general message to the group that what counts are as many unusual, interesting, and novel ideas as possible. We tend to use it with groups of young people for career planning, in order to start expanding their horizons. We also use it with cross-cultural groups who are sharing English as an international language, some of whose members have a greater command of the language than others. We find the game useful for integrating and developing language skills.

We form groups of five to seven people. Each group forms itself into a circle and is then asked to produce a volunteer to be 'brainstormed' with helpful ideas from group members on any topic the volunteer suggests. We spend a few moments with each volunteer discussing possible problems they might like some help with. We do not hesitate to be fairly directive at this stage because the real business of the game is yet to come.

Now we ask each team to select a reporter, and then announce the rule that nobody shall criticize anybody else's ideas. No matter how crazy the ideas may sound, the participants should just keep them coming. All ideas will be recorded by each group's reporter and discussed later. If the volunteer is a youngster in high school, maybe the brainstorm will be about what kind of career he or she might pursue. If the participants are there to learn English, volunteers might like to be brainstormed with ways to improve their pronunciation, gain a larger vocabulary, increase their ability to agree or disagree in English, and generally gain more confidence in speaking the language.

The various reporters write all the ideas in coloured felt-tipped pens on newsprint. (Give each reporter a different coloured pen, if you can.) The reporters can write on the floor, in the middle of the circle, or their team can huddle with them round a table.

Give all the brainstormers a couple of minutes to confirm the topic on which they are going to bombard the volunteer with ideas, and be prepared to wander round from group to group with more helpful ideas, if necessary. Then give everybody about five to seven minutes — more if they are buzzing with ideas — before announcing that the inventive phase of the game is over and the evaluation about to begin. Each group now goes back over all of their ideas, narrowing them down to one or two that really appeal to their respective volunteers, and elaborating on them as they see fit.

Then there is a final, plenary, phase in which each group takes it in turn to describe to the whole class what happened in their group. Time all this carefully or it will take hours: five minutes for explaining the game, three minutes for getting the players into their group circles and selecting reporters and volunteers, five minutes for general discussion about topics that the volunteer would like brainstormed, five to ten minutes for brainstorming, five minutes for refining the ideas, ten to 15 minutes for the plenary session — perhaps three-quarters of an hour altogether unless you have a really large class.

Played like this, 'Brainstorm' can have some surprising results. On one occasion, one of the volunteers was a teacher who elected to be brainstormed on other careers he might follow apart from teaching. He was part of a group of teachers who entered into the spirit of the exercise with empathy and imagination; he was brainstormed until his head was spinning. When he reported to the plenary session on the experience, he said: 'I didn't realize until now just how miserable I am as a teacher. This exercise hasn't taught me what it is I want to do next, but it has shown me what I definitely *don't* want to do!'

On another occasion, also a career planning seminar, a teenage volunteer said that nobody had been able to come up with any career that she really felt she would like to follow. Her group members (her high school colleagues) were clearly frustrated by the whole experience and we were about to pitch in with encouraging reassurances when she said: 'Of course . . . what I'd *really* like to do . . .' 'Yes, yes, what is it?' her team-mates urged her. 'What I'd really like to do . . . is be a cook!' The interesting thing was that a cook was just about the only job that the brainstormers had not thought of, and that Theresa had not mentioned, until now. Apparently, the exercise had started her thinking and she was able to take it from there. We are happy to report that she went to technical college and trained as a cook, and that we were invited to her graduation — which included a magnificent lunch cooked by the graduates.

We know another little warm-up, called 'Thumbs Up', that we are rather fond of. It offers useful clues to individuals' motivations.

'Thumbs Up'

Ask everyone to put both hands out in front at arm's length. The easiest way to explain this is for you to demonstrate it physically. Then ask them to clasp their hands together and to note which thumb is on top (you can wriggle your own thumb in illustration). Next instruct them to put their hands down by their sides, and then, as quickly as they can, to re-clasp their hands out in front of them with the *other* thumb on top.

Wait a moment for the experience to sink in. Never be afraid of silence when you are playing a game. It can be one of your most effective tools — whether you want to emphasize something, to initiate discussion (by putting psychological pressure on the group to break the silence), or to draw attention to something that has happened or to something someone has said. You can use silence as a punishment, as we noted earlier, or as a reward. Respectful silence can be a tribute paid by you to a participant who has just said something particularly insightful, before you draw the group's attention to it.

Back to 'Thumbs Up'. Ask people now to fold their arms across their chests, and then, very quickly, to re-fold them *the other way*. Then ask everyone to turn to their neighbour and tell that person *how they felt* during the exercise. Give everyone a few minutes to do this. You may have to help them at the start, for instance, by indicating to someone who their 'neighbour' is, putting the occasional threesome together if one person does not seem to have a partner, and so on.

Listen to the noise level. It will probably build as people get into their stride, peak, and begin to descend. Wait until most people seem to have stopped talking and are obviously expecting you to do something. In strongly people-oriented groups the buzz of talk will go for ages. If the chatter gives no sign of abating by itself, give it, say, five minutes at the most and then collect everyone's attention. High problem-solvers tend to be quieter than people-oriented players but even if there is almost no discussion do not become unnerved — wait for at least two or three minutes without saying anything more, even if by now there is complete silence in the room (though take courage, we have never known this to happen).

Then ask the class as a whole for feedback. Ask them to repeat aloud some of the remarks they were making to each other, for you to post on the board. There may be some hesitation, but if you stand there, waiting, with the chalk in your hand, sooner or later someone will call out something like 'Awkward', which will start the ball rolling.

It is most important that you do not prompt anyone at this stage, though if the group is exceptionally quiet you could ask one or two leading questions, like: 'Did anyone dislike it?' Someone will probably either say 'yes', or some form of qualified yes, and then you can ask: 'In what way?' and so on, until people give you *their* noun or adjective to describe what they felt ('Well, I felt such a fool!' or 'I didn't like it because I didn't understand the point of the exercise!').

If the group is large and mixed, you will get some wide variations in responses, such as 'It shows the power of habit.'; 'It was fun, I love doing things like that!'; and 'I wondered what was the point of the whole thing.' Post them all, in summary (but get the speakers to agree to the summary and do not replace their words with yours unless *they* think your words are better).

When everyone has had time to contemplate this feedback for a while, introduce them to the idea that nobody sees the same task or problem in quite the same way. For instance, some people will be more inclined to interpret it in terms of human feelings and relationships because those are the things that interest them most; others tend to see problems as challenges to their ingenuity; still others are more inclined to solve the problem or accomplish the task by use of power (over themselves or other people). If they cannot fit the problem or task into their particular framework, they are likely to lack motivation to solve or accomplish it.

The evidence for what motivates individual group members is in the comments that you have recorded. 'I felt funny' is a feelings-oriented statement and different in kind from something like: 'I was afraid I wasn't doing it right', which can be interpreted as a complaint about the speaker's sense of powerlessness or lack of control of the situation. A remark such as 'What's the point?' suggests either that the individual is attempting to question the authority of the game leader or that the questioner wants to retain control of his or her own thinking processes — or perhaps both. On the other hand, the questioner may be indicating a less personal and more abstract response, perhaps implying a deductive or convergent need: 'What conclusion can I draw from this experience?'

Everyone is capable of being motivated by combinations of needs for power and people and problem-solving, and, no doubt, the need that is uppermost in any one individual at any one time will depend on a great many complexities and circumstances, some of which the person can control and some of which are part of the larger environment. Nevertheless, people do appear to develop (or to possess from birth) a *propensity* towards one kind of motivation rather than another. Some people seem to like playing power games more than others, for example. *Why* they feel the need to do so is another matter, and not within the scope of this book. The point is that your participants should understand that these patterns exist and begin to recognize inside themselves the kinds of problems and situations that most motivate them — if they are to develop effective leadership styles.

One of your responsibilities is to help the participants learn to work as a group, rather than as a collection of isolated individuals, for groups generate their own learning, and — according to the law of averages, if nothing else — the group knows more than you do about almost everything. Your job as leader is to release the learning power of the group, which should go far beyond your input to levels and dimensions that you could never bring them to by yourself. When this begins to happen the line between 'teacher' and 'learner' disappears altogether. The roles become interchangeable and you and the group continually negotiate meanings between you — and group members between each other — in a dynamic burst of mental energy that is often called synergy. This process occurs when any teaching method has been effectively used, but with gaming it seems to be enhanced. It can generate an intellectual 'high' in everybody, and however exhausted you are by the end of the session, you are wiser than when you began because you have shared the learning of the group.

There is a game called 'Broken Squares' (Pfeiffer·and Jones, 1975), which we play to demonstrate the kind of autonomy that people have to surrender if they want to benefit from the advantages of being members of a working team. We have come across several versions of this game in other publications, but this is how we play it.

'Broken Squares'

Obtain some thick cardboard (we have cut our puzzle pieces out of wood and painted them in lots of bright colours. If you are going to

use this game a lot, we suggest that you do the same). Draw the
outlines of the pieces, measuring their dimensions carefully with a
ruler. Cut out the pieces and put them together in five little packages
as described in the Appendix on pp. 156-7. If your groups consists of
about seven to ten people you need only one set, ie five packages
(which will contain a total of 15 pieces in all) for five players; the
rest of the group can be observers. If you have a lot of players — over
30, for example — you will need six sets, and so on. Do not worry
too much if you do not have any observers in large groups because
one set of five players is sure to finish before the others and then you
can ask them to observe the struggles of the remaining players.

The only rules are: no talking at all, and no taking of or asking for
other people's pieces, by force or non-verbal persuasion. If you like,
you can supply the information that all of the completed squares
will be approximately six inches in diameter, but you may not want
to provide any clues at all, in which case the game will take longer —
anything from ten minutes to half an hour.

Each of the five players in any given set begins with a few odd
pieces of a puzzle, and each must end with a complete square iden-
tical in size with those of the others, that is, five squares in all.
It looks impossible at first; the only way it can be done is for the
players to stop thinking as individuals and operate as members of
a team.

We saw this demonstrated in an amazing way once, when we
played 'Broken Squares' with a group of teachers. As soon as the
pieces are distributed, it becomes obvious that some players cannot
make a square with what they have, but one of these teachers took
this observation to its logical conclusion faster than we have ever
seen anybody do it. He threw his brightly coloured wooden pieces
with a clatter into the middle of the table and indicated so forcefully in pantomime that the others should do so too that they did,
though uncomprehendingly at first. He soon made it clear by his
actions that the five squares were to be built out of the common
supply, and they were completed very quickly. This was an unusually
neat demonstration of what happens when you get a confident,
authoritative leader imposing a sense of direction and purpose on
team-members, who can then take over and complete the task in
record time.

Other patterns emerge from building 'Broken Squares'. What
commonly happens is that one player completes what looks like a
good square; in fact, the player has used too many pieces and the
other four squares cannot be made out of what is left. Often the
owner does not realize this for a while and neither do the other four
players, who continue to move their own and eventually other
people's pieces around without getting anywhere. Meanwhile, the

square-holder sits there, an interested and sympathetic outsider, observing the team. Sooner or later it dawns on the players that the original square will have to be broken up and the whole thing started again; but how are they to communicate this to its owner? Sometimes the owner becomes aware of this quite quickly, and willingly breaks up the square. Others take much longer to grasp the situation and are much more reluctant to give up their personal possessions. This happens with all age groups, as far as we have observed. Young children can be very possessive of their toys but so can grown ups. A colleague of ours reports having seen a bank manager hang on to his square, oblivious to the needs of his team, until the frustration level was so high — not only in his group but in our colleague — that she was literally sitting on her hands to stop herself leaning over the man's shoulder and breaking up his square by force.

What players can learn experientially from this game is that there are restrictions imposed on people who want to be part of a team. They have to give up some of their personal power in order to complete a task for which they need the help of the group. So long as tasks continue to be accomplished and comradeship is strong, leaders will be prepared to surrender autonomy and to pace themselves to the needs of the group, and followers will refrain from mutiny.

Another short game that illustrates this need to put group needs before one's own is 'To Be Or Not . . .'

'To Be Or Not . . .'

Ask everyone to form groups of six to ten people and then to stand or sit in a circle or a square. If there are lots of people, form two or more circles. Give any one individual in each of the circles the word 'To'; then give the word 'be' to the person beside them; and so on until the six people respectively have been given the words 'To-be-or-not-to-be', one word at a time. With the larger circle you add the words 'That-is-the-question', again as single words, or two words, to each player.

Now ask them to say their words out loud, in turn. The first person will start off tentatively or boldly, as the case may be, saying 'To.' Note that we have written a full stop after the word to give a sense of how the player is likely to say it. The next speaker, realizing it is his or her turn, will say: 'Be!'

This process will continue until everybody has had their turn. The result almost invariably is a collection of disconnected words uttered at random. Then you rehearse the group several times until they learn to listen empathetically to each other, pick up the previous speaker's word, add their own, and pass the combination on to the next in line so that the whole sentence assumes rhythm and meaning. It is also a very good exercise for improving people's concentration.

You do not have to use Shakespeare — a prose passage from a book or newspaper will do just as well. You can write your own — perhaps with some subtleties, as in: 'Look out! Oh, dear; I *did* warn you about the puddle! Are you *very* wet?' which requires the speakers to decide on the ordering of information and to adopt a number of different intonations, depending on different meanings and the intentions of the speaker.

There is another game, similar in organization and concept, that also enhances concentration and empathy, which we call 'Simultaneous Interpretation'.

'Simultaneous Interpretation'

With five to seven players sitting in a circle, ask one player to read aloud continuously from a book or newspaper. Then ask the person on the reader's right to repeat every word, the second they hear it, to the next listener and so on round the circle until it all gets back to the reader. With a bit of practice, teams can become so skilful that their readers will hear their own words repeated in their ears like echoes of their own voices.

Foreign language interpreters can become so fast with their translations that they are known as 'simultaneous interpreters', which is where we got the name for this game. These translators appear to develop a rapid and almost intuitive rapport with a speaker, even somebody with whom they have not worked before, so that it really seems as if they know what will be said before the words leave the speaker's mouth. Your game players are not being asked to translate what they hear into another language (though that might be another useful game), merely to repeat what they hear. This exercise can easily be adapted to increase fluency in speaking and understanding a foreign tongue, and players will not find it very difficult to develop the concentration and empathy that make this such an effective game.

Now we want to describe three more good games: short preliminary exercises that can be played as introductions to theoretical parts of a seminar or course (or later, to illustrate the theory). The first we call 'Roger's Game' because a man named Roger first described it to us. It is helpful in illustrating the power of leaders to get their followers to behave in ways they might not normally choose. Then there is 'Either . . . Or', which is about personal choices, and 'Status', which concerns people's value-judgements and the ways in which people attribute power to others.

'Roger's Game'

This takes about ten minutes to play, but the players should be given plenty of time to talk about it afterwards — which is true for all games. We cannot stress too strongly that people must be encouraged to talk at length about what happened to them during a gaming session. If you have a time problem, cut down on the time spent playing, and not on the debriefing.

'Roger's Game' is suitable for classroom environments where there are not too many people (30 is probably about the top limit) and where there is space for each individual in turn to come up to the blackboard. Announce that this is a game about winning and losing, and then take five, ten, or 20 pence from each player to put into a common fund for prize money. If group members are very wealthy — senior business people, for example — you may be able to squeeze them for 50 pence or a pound each.

Usually the more money there is in the fund, the better motivated are the players. However, if you are working with a cross-cultural group, remember that some members may have very conservative views about playing games for money. In these circumstances it might be better to provide the prize yourself in the form of something like multi-coloured sweets.

Now draw on the board a matrix of six squares by six, ie 36 squares. Then pick two people in the class to be team leaders. You will get the most visible results if you select participants whom you have already decided are competitive in temperament, which is why 'Roger's Game' is best played when you know your players reasonably well. Use words such as 'team-member' and 'leader' to encourage a spirit of competition.

Ask the leaders to pick their teams by taking turns to select one person from the group until everyone has been chosen. Toss a coin to decide who chooses first. If there is one person left over at the end, that person becomes umpire. If numbers are even, then you are the umpire. Appear to be taking all of these preliminaries very seriously.

When the teams are made up, give one leader a stick of coloured chalk and the other leader a piece of chalk of a different colour. Tell everyone that the game is to play a version of 'Noughts and Crosses', or 'Tic-Tac-Toe'. In Roger's version, team-members take turns to make either a zero or a cross on the board. There will be 10 turns altogether, and the object is for each team to get as many complete rows as they can, horizontally or vertically, of zeros or crosses as the case may be.

Repeat this information as often as you need but do not say any more about the objectives of the game. Tell everyone that each completed row will win 20 pence for the successful team (or 50 pence, a pound or 50 sweets, depending on what is in the pot). Suggest that leaders brief their teams and give them a few minutes to discuss strategies, which you may find they do in whispers so the rival team cannot hear them.

Then each team-member has 15 seconds to approach the board, make the relevant cross or zero, and return to hand the chalk to their next team-mate; and so on, each team marking the board alternately until all the turns have been completed. Start counting the seconds out loud if anyone is slow to move. Keep up the pace and pressure, to increase the suspense.

We have played this game dozens of times, with a great variety of learning groups, and it is almost always played competitively. That is, at least one member of each team will deliberately prevent the other team from completing a row. Usually the saboteurs are given verbal encouragement by their team-mates. The usual result is either that no one wins a prize or that someone makes a mistake in the excitement of the moment and allows one line to be completed. If this happens, we duly hand over a prize.

Then we point out that theoretically the maximum number of lines that can be completed up and down the board is three by one team and three by another, which would yield a reasonable prize for both teams; however, this can happen only if both teams cooperate. So what do the words 'to win' and 'to lose' mean? Is winning a zero-sum affair in which winning means inevitably that someone else has to lose? Be prepared for some resistance to this argument at first. It will come as a surprise — even a shock — to some of the players that there should be any doubt about the matter, particularly if they are Australian or American business people. 'Of course!', they will say: 'You have to beat your competitors!'

You may have to get your message across by offering such suggestions as: 'You may win more often with other people's help'; and: 'Other people will help you if they can see something in it for themselves'. You can support this rather manipulative argument by discussing with the players the strategies that you used to 'set them up' for 'Roger's Game', as follows:

(1) Your *assessment* of some players as being more competitive by temperament than others, and choosing them to be team leaders on that basis.

(2) Your apparent *assumption* that the game was competitive, which directed players to see it that way without question.

(3) Your *time-management* of the game so players were given little chance to think of alternative strategies.

(4) The kind of *motivation* that you employed, ie 'prizes for the winners', which predisposed the teams to think in terms of beating their opponents.

(5) Your *progression* through the whole exercise, in a linear, logical, step-by-step way that concealed its built-in assumptions.

Therefore, without the players realizing it, their decision-making was not based on objective criteria, but on how you, their leader, described the problem

If you should come across a group that refuses to 'play your game', and the teams decide to cooperate instead of working against each other (though we have seldom had this experience), discuss with them why your leadership was not effective. You can learn a lot about your leadership style from their answers.

'Either... Or'

This is a game to help people increase their awareness of how they make choices — by recognizing some of the influences that make them decide to do one thing and not another, which is an essential component in understanding how leaders lead and why followers follow. It takes about 20 minutes to play and follows very appropriately after any static activity in which participants have been sitting at their desks or tables for some time. Any number can play, but either the furniture must be moveable or there must be some other empty space available, like a hall, foyer, lounge, or even the yard.

Ask everyone to stand in a line down the middle of the room. Tell them that you are going to ask them some questions which they are to answer by moving three paces to the left or to the right, or by staying where they are. The first set of questions is:

'Are you Yesterday? (If so, move to the left)';
'Are you Today? (Stay where you are)';
'Or are you Tomorrow? (Move to the right)'.

Repeat the questions several times if needed. Note that you are asking the players to identify themselves with all of the accrued meanings that they personally attach to each of the words. There may be some initial puzzlement, after which a few people — maybe more — will step to the left or right. Wait until everybody seems to have made a decision and then ask the players, in turn, why they phone to move one way or the other, or to stay in the centre line. As they explain (perhaps they are Yesterdays because of their love of the past — old customs, buildings, etc), one or two others may leave the centre and move to either the left or the right, as they realize what is expected of them.

You can think of any number of 'either . . . ors' for yourself, but here are a few suggestions: Are you:

a wordprocessor? (Move to the left);
a gold fountain pen? (Move to the right);
or a simple lead pencil? (Stay where you are).

a sign that says, 'Open to visitors'? (Move to the left);
a sign that says, 'No trespassers'? (Move to the right);
or a sign that says, 'Back in one hour'? (Stay where you are).

a mountain? (Move to the left);
a valley? (Move to the right);
or a plain? (Stay where you are).

the earth? (Move to the left);
the sea? (Move to the right);
or the sky? (Stay where you are).

the city? (Move to the left);
the country? (Move to the right);
or the suburbs? (Stay where you are).

Yes? (Move to the left);
No? (Move to the right);
or Maybe? (Stay where you are).

Our favourite 'either . . . or' is: 'Are you a Volkswagen? a Rolls Royce? or something else?'. The reasons that people give for being one of these, or another kind of car altogether, like a four-wheel drive or a convertible, reveal a lot about themselves. They say things like: 'I'm a VW because I'm reliable, economical and safe!'; or: 'I just kind of like the whole concept of being a Rolls Royce — the power, the luxury; it's being a cut above the rest!'; or: 'I'm a Jeep because it reminds me of camping in the mountains'.

Encourage the participants to ask one another questions about their choices. The explanations are always interesting, the listeners find them informative, and the whole process is likely to increase self-awareness and understanding of one's own and other's motivations.

The final game in this section is another in which the players have to move about the room, this time in order to create visible opinion-polls.

'Status'

With any group of players, brainstorm them to write a list of occupations that they might consider working in, all things being equal. One list, created by a somewhat tongue-in-cheek group of university undergraduates, included the following:

Systems analyst
Millionaire
Landscape architect
Garbage collector
Lawyer
Dole bludger (this is a derogatory term used by establishment
    Australians to describe people who live on welfare)
Prison warder
Town planner
Laundry attendant
Tax evader
Social worker
Football player
Catholic priest
Pediatrician
Teacher

From this list, write each occupation on a separate label of some kind, preferably the sort that you can stick on people's foreheads or somewhere else highly visible. Label all the players at random with one of these stickers and ask them to move around and read each other's occupations. Then ask them to form a line down the centre of the room in order of status, with the person whose occupation is highest in status at the head. Tell them that they have 10 minutes (or 15, or even longer if the group is large and vocal). After that, do not get involved at all; pass all questions back to the group. Stress that it does not matter by what criteria they choose to define 'status'. It is up to them to form the line any way they want. You may have to urge them along a bit by emphasizing the deadline or suggesting at which end of the room the head of the line should stand, but eventually you will probably see an uneven straggle of people, some of them still arguing about who stands in front of whom. Tidy them up a bit ('You're a nurse. Do you think your status is higher than that of this sales clerk? Well, then, you stand in front of him like this!').

Now initiate discussion about the order of rank. How and why did it come about? The kind of information that you want to reveal without asking for it directly is whether a person's attitude towards a particular occupation created a self-fulfilling prophecy about the status of that occupation. Did players' occupations affect their own behaviour and the behaviour of others towards them? For example, in American society the occupation of 'Pediatrician' is high-income and high-status. Did the player labelled 'Pediatrician' have any problems getting to the head of the line or near it? Did that player *expect* to have any problems? On the other hand, if a player was labelled 'Garbage collector', did that person end up near the bottom of the line? If so, did they dispute it, or accept it as appropriate? What about professions such as 'Teacher' and 'Social Worker'? Where did they end up in the line? Did anybody offer any criteria for status that were not based on money?

In our experience, 'Status' is most effectively played with cross-cultural groups, groups of political activists, groups of players who in real life belong to disadvantaged minorities, and groups of very senior executives (though trying to stick labels on senior executives' foreheads is a status game in itself). Different groups come up with very different lists, and the game always seems to cause a lot of interested — sometimes heated — debate about personal values versus the opinions of society; and about status, money and power.

This brings to an end our chapter on warm-ups and triggers. Some readers may be interested to know how we designed these short games; we have therefore included this information in the next chapter.

Designing and Selecting Games to Trigger Learning

If you are interested in playing short games, either as 'warm-ups' with your students or as 'triggers' to activate their thinking on a particular topic, you should always be on the alert for ideas that you can shape into a game. The exercises in the previous chapter are examples of simple games whose design can be inspired by almost anything — reading a novel, seeing a movie, or listening to an anecdote at a party. In our experience, the most productive ideas come from stories, movies, plays and television, that is, from fiction. Fiction writers, dramatists and story-tellers have to shape their living material in order to give it structure and meaning — which is what you have to do when you create a game. If you adapt a fictional (or narrated) idea, situation or event into a game, some of your work will have already been done for you by the author.

With experience, you can also adapt virtually any existing longer game that you hear about or get out of a book. You can simplify it, rearrange it, and generally cut up its organization, thus tailoring it to your specific needs. The criteria that you should keep in mind are as follows:

(1) The game activity must be — or you must be able to make it — relevant to the rest of your material. Thus, if you teach natural sciences to high school students you can take a basic 'structured experience' like 'The Body Machine' — a game that encourages imaginative group improvisation, in which the players create a 'moving picture' using their bodies as the functioning parts — and turn it into a strategy for learning about the process of digestion in the human body. We describe how we did this on pp. 62-4 (in the game called 'Down it Goes!').

(2) The game should aim specifically to illustrate one basic theme. Of course, it will provide examples of a range of human emotions and behaviour, because the actions of human beings are the raw material from which the game is made, but your debriefing of necessity, has to be selective. It has to focus only on comparisons and contrasts in players' behaviour that relate directly to your

subject matter — which means you have to be very observant of players' responses. Therefore, you do not want to create a great deal of general and irrelevant activity because you will not be able to take it all in.

(3) The game should be product-oriented, and involve people in conflict. These are the ingredients for ensuring dramatic content. The players need to become involved in some visible problem-solving activity, preferably where there is a *product*, like the answer to a puzzle or any sort of outcome that can be evaluated and used as a criterion by which to examine the action. You may find it useful to remember that one definition of drama is 'people in conflict'. This does not mean that the players have got to start fighting each other, or that there need by any kind of aggression. The conflict may be a dialectic between one idea and another that creates something new: thesis — antithesis — synthesis.

The more dramatic the game is, within reason, the more likely it is to evoke highly visible results. This is one of the reasons why we suggested earlier that you should occasionally videotape games, so you can watch how people have reacted to a particular game, in order to help you make it more effective in the future.

To compare games, ie 'structured experiences', to drama is to suggest that they contain the potential to surprise, even shock, the participants. To use another metaphor, in a sense they are explosive devices, though their detonations usually stimulate players' amusement, curiosity, interest and surprise rather than deeper emotions. However, it is important to remember that you are playing with dynamite. Surprise can quickly turn to outrage, amusement to derision and hostility, and curiosity to rejection. Do not make the mistake of thinking that players cannot become upset by short and simple games. People's responses to experiential material are always complex and, however elementary the game, you have to be quick on your feet to control the results.

To illustrate these points, we want to take you in some detail through an experience of a game we invented as a warm-up for a management training session on leader legitimacy. The players found their own and each others' responses so thought-provoking that the game became a sort of touchstone against which to test the rest of the session for 'truth'. But in spite of its effectiveness, and although it was designed to meet all of the criteria listed above, the response of one player made us aware that the game can be explosive.

The seminar was about acquiring confidence — self-legitimacy — in leadership roles. One of us had read a sentence somewhere in a novel about a character worrying about what to wear because he was anxious about giving 'the right impression'. This started us thinking about the clothes leaders choose to wear. So we collected some props — a suede jacket, a fur coat, a few scarves, hats, gloves, bangles, baubles, beads — anything that looked dramatic and expensive, and we invented a game called 'Who's the Leader?'

'Who's the Leader?'

We divided the class into four groups of five people each, gave each group in turn the whole set of props, and sent them out of the room for a few minutes to dress up as 'leaders', any way they wanted, individually or as a group. When they came back into the room the rest of us had to guess what kind of leaders they were. It turned out to be a good game because several players got right into the spirit of the thing and the observers were supportive and asked constructive questions. One 'actor' wore the fur coat and then announced that he was a union representative (which in fact he was in real life). When his audience commented that he looked more like a capitalist, he said that he wanted to demonstrate his egalitarian principles. Why should not workers be dressed as luxuriously as their bosses?

Most of the other players — who, remember, were all managers in real life — disdained to wear any articles of costume and insisted their own suits were appropriate for the status of a leader. (Note for inexperienced game leaders: there's no need to panic if players do not do what you ask them. Work with them, not against them. If the game is supposed to be about dressing up, like this one, and they will not dress up, do not worry; ask them why they do not think the costume articles are appropriate. Keep the questions respectful, impersonal, non-threatening, and pertinent to the exercise.)

The whole game lasted less than half an hour but everybody seemed to get a kick out of it. It resulted in a discussion that ran for nearly an hour about clothes as devices to legitimize and demonstrate the power of the wearer. Participants showed each other some of the articles they habitually wore (like a very expensive and elaborate wristwatch) as status symbols. The men in particular talked about other possessions as symbols of power, including cars, houses and beautiful women. We were able later to extend this line of thought to explore some of the power symbols that women have traditionally adopted, what kind of power these symbols suggested, and what strategies today's professional women managers might adopt to demonstrate their legitimacy as leaders. And so on.

So far, so good. We had designed a game in which the participants did highly visible things. Players confronted the audience in a dramatic and problem-solving activity that produced results which could be evaluated in terms of the given problem. These responses could then be related in debriefing back to the core material of the course for which this was the warm-up, thus ensuring that the whole course was enriched by the creative input of its participants.

However, there was a dangerous fly in the ointment. One man had apparently found it very funny that another male player should have chosen during the role-play, to wear a double row of pearls, high heeled shoes, and make-up. He kept laughing and making rude remarks at the idea of the actor being in the role of a female managing director. This observer found it difficult, when the actual seminar got under way, to relate appropriately to the man who had assumed the role. He kept making suggestive remarks, which everyone resented.

The group assumed (and we privately agreed) that the joker had some motive relating to his own sexuality which led him to overreact to the dressing-up game. Because this was not a therapy session, we could not allow the group dynamic to founder over one participant's personal problems. Therefore, we boldly grasped the nettle, introduced the topic of leadership and sexuality, and discussed ways in which leaders — men and women — can manage to legitimize their sexuality as human beings and yet avoid unwanted sexual complications in the workplace. We kept the whole discussion on an academic level with no reference to the warm-up, and it was received as such by all the participants after a certain amount of initial embarrassment. The topic was a useful addition to the course which we would not have thought of under ordinary circumstances, and there was no further problem with the trouble-maker.

The whole experience of this playing of 'Who's the Leader?' (which was almost too dramatic for our comfort; we are glad to report that nothing like it has happened on subsequent occasions when we have played it) illustrates the risks and gains of gaming for learning. Game leaders have to be confident — that is, they must have a good command of their professional material and must be able to trust their leadership skills, even if they are not trained teachers. They must respond continually to feedback from the group — in other words, they must be prepared to learn continuously from the group and adapt their behaviour according to what they learn. The return for this kind of investment is the virtual certainty that the participants will receive a powerful experience that they can relate directly and profitably to their professional lives and that will come to mean even more to them in hindsight.

If you find the concept of 'Who's the Leader?' attractive, but too dramatic, there is a much less dramatic version you could try, which usually evokes an interesting discussion. We call it 'Identikit'.

'Identikit'

Assemble from newspapers and magazines a number of close-ups and full-length photographs of men and women. It does not matter who they are, or what they are doing. Get as many as you can and as wide a variety as you can. Then spread the whole lot out in front of your students and ask each of them to assemble a collage on the personality of an international leader — for example, the Prime Minister of India, the King of Thailand, or the President of the United States — asking the students to select as many photographs as they need in order to represent what they think are the key facets of this public leader's personality. For example, a student might decide that one person's trademarks are her wide-eyed stare, her rather strident voice, and her middle-class, establishment appearance. Therefore, this student might assemble a collage of photographs depicting people with staring eyes, pictures of people shouting (or close-ups of mouths), and people wearing conservative clothes.

The easiest way to explain this game to a group is to make up a collage yourself in advance, to serve as a model. In making it, you will quickly find what sort of photos you need, and therefore what you should provide for your players. Then explain your identikit to the group before asking each of them to make his or her own. You will find that participants enjoy this game, once they get the hang of it. Their biggest problem is likely to be that the photographs they are being asked to work with are not those of the personalities themselves — many people have very literal minds. However, as soon as they realize that they are to look for characteristics in the portraits that they think their chosen leader shares, they are off and away. When all the collages have been assembled, the artists pass them around for comments and congratulations; then you initiate a discussion about leadership styles, based on the data of the identikits, which are frequently quite awe-inspiring in their originality.

There is another aspect of designing games that we should discuss, and that is the provision of game materials. We have already advised you to 'keep it simple' when you set out to create a game, and this advice applies also to its materials. The two examples above — of costume props and photographs respectively — will require a lot of your time and imagination to collect but they are not complicated or difficult. We find ourselves almost automatically rejecting games that we read about or hear about if they require a long list of supplies. If games can be compared to drama and described as 'people in conflict', they can also borrow a metaphor from the theatre: 'two planks and passion'. In other words, a game, like a play, need be no more than an empty room across which some people move while others watch them.

Metaphors can be carried too far, but this one may serve to illustrate that the players' actions and feelings are paramount in games, not the materials. Therefore, as a general rule, it is best to use what you have at hand when you design games and use your imagination to make them appropriate to your needs. Virtually anything can become game material. To give you an example, the following is a game we designed during a conference for educators, on simulation games, in Melbourne some years ago. It is the most complicated design we have to offer in this chapter but it was truly a 'trigger' in the context of the conference and it confirms our point about using what you have got.

We had been asked to give an *ad hoc* demonstration of game design and were inspired by the fact that one of the conference rooms in the hotel could be turned into a ballroom by the simple device of removing the carpet, which was laid on the floor in large squares. We watched a man come in one evening with a pushcart, load all the squares on to it, and wheel it away — and we promptly sat down and devised a game we called 'Ponsonby' because that was the name of the hotel.

'Ponsonby'

The goals of this game are virtually the same as for 'Roger's Game', which we described in the last chapter: to examine how individual perceptions about a group task can affect the end result, and to study the effects of competitive behaviour on group perceptions of the task. We played it at the conference with over 100 people in the large hall, using the carpet squares that we have described. We are aware that the likelihood of your being able to reproduce this situation is remote. Therefore, we offer this anecdote merely as an illustration of how to take advantage of your environment to create structured experiences for your students.

We warned a couple of people in advance that we were going to ask them to coach players for a team game, though we did not tell them what the game was. We asked them to instruct their team-members, when the time came, as follows:

(1) The coach for Team A has to urge the team to win at all costs. It is to be impressed on them that this is a competitive situation and they are in it to win, even if this involves a certain amount of aggression — within the rules — towards the opposing team.

(2) The coach for Team B is to stress that the object of this game is to study group processes, and that it has been designed purely as light relief in an otherwise demanding conference. The object is

to observe players' behaviour during the course of the game, and to enjoy the game; never mind about the result.

When the time came to demonstrate the game to the conference, we moved everybody into the hall. The carpet squares, with the permission of the functions manager, had been arranged in advance. Half the squares were placed in heaps in a line along one wall of the room, the other half along the opposite wall, revealing the expanse of parquet flooring. We divided the parquet down the middle lengthwise with a chalk line, got everybody into two teams — one team to line up against one wall, the other team against the opposite wall. Thus the two teams faced each other across the room, a pile of carpet squares along the wall behind each team, and a chalk line on a bare floor between them

We asked them to imagine that they were two sporting teams who were to play against each other. The two coaches then took charge and privately gave their respective teams the prepared briefings. When the coaches were satisfied that their teams had been sufficiently motivated, we explained that the object of the game was to carpet the floor. The rules were that Team A members had to cross the floor, pick up the squares that were lined up behind Team B — one square per person at a time — recross the room, and start laying the squares from their own side of the room up to the chalk line. Team B had to do the same with the squares behind Team A.

This meant that all the players were continually crossing and recrossing the room, each person picking up a carpet square from one side of the room, carrying it across, laying it on their own team's territory and then repeating the process. As one might expect, the team who thought they were playing a competitive game began rushing to and fro as fast as they could, laying squares at a very fast rate, while the non-competitive team members collected their squares very casually, watching the other team with surprised interest. After a few moments, however, the dynamic changed. The frenetic activity of Team A began to communicate itself to Team B, especially as Team A's members were visibly and audibly gloating over their superior performance. Before long, the game turned into a race in which — because players from the opposing teams were crossing into each other's territory all the time — there was a lot of pushing and shoving.

As the floor became more and more carpeted, Team A looked certain to win because they had been competitive from the beginning — but then the going started getting rougher. One woman from Team B stood on a square to prevent a Team A man from picking it up. The man lifted her physically off her feet, none too gently, dumped her down on the floor, and picked up the square. From then on, that woman became one of the most aggressive players, but none of her team-mates were far behind her. In fact, Team B ended up being noticeably more belligerent than Team A, and 'won' the game.

During the debriefing the woman described how she had begun 'Ponsonby' in a relaxed and contented frame of mind — grateful to it for giving her 'time out' from mental effort. She ended the game, she said, feeling that she would have killed to win, and feeling deeply resentful that she should have been 'made' to feel this way by the offensive behaviour of Team A. All of the members of Team B expressed similar feelings and all blamed their feelings on Team A for being so 'pushy and horrible'. Team A at first could not see what all the fuss was about — which effectively opened up the debate along the lines of our objectives for the game.

'Ponsonby' was the highlight of the conference, and people talked about it all week. It had been a serendipitous combination of the three components of gaming: the people, the setting and the game. The game structure was dramatic — conflict of desires, reversal of expectations, action and suspense — and well suited to its objectives and the needs of the players. And all because we happened to see a man picking up carpet squares off a floor.

Now let's get back to the concept of drama being 'two planks and passion', the notion of games as dramatic learning strategies, and the suggestion that a game's director and players can generate all the learning material they need without any outside help at all. For example, you can invent an imaginative exercise like the following.

'My Car Won't Start'

Imagine that you are already late for an important appointment some distance away. You get into your car, but it will not start. What is the *first thing* you do?

Players answer this question in a variety of ways and, of course, there is no 'right' or 'wrong' answer — which is something you keep telling participants when you are playing games with them. However, the answers to little guessing games like this can provide useful clues to the problem-solving styles of the respondents and, as we have already said, this is information that you need in order to do your job.

Some people reply immediately that they would try to fix the car (or the moped, bicycle, or whatever you have specified. If you are working with students from China, for example, the vehicle would probably be a bicycle). This experimental attitude (ie one that seeks to test theoretical knowledge by using it to solve practical problems) is quite different from behaviour that first seeks a telephone or to send a message in some way to change or cancel the appointment. The latter answer implies a sense of future, of the need to plan. Other players are 'here and now' people who turn first neither to their own theoretical knowledge nor to the future but to the help that they can get from their present environment. Their suggestions might include begging, borrowing, or stealing some alternative form of transport. They would 'hitch a lift'; 'call a friend'; or 'borrow my spouse's car' (presumably, whether the spouse needs it or not).

This problem-solving style requires good powers of persuasion in individualistic cultures where you are supposed to solve your own problems all by yourself — like those of Britain and America, for example — but less so in countries like Japan. A Japanese business-man on a management training course once told us that in this situation in real life he would stand in the middle of the street and stop any car, asking the driver to take him to his destination. This reply was culture-specific; we could not imagine him getting away with it in Sydney or New York or London, and we were very much impressed that he took it for granted he could do so in Tokyo. Nevertheless, it indicated a problem-solving style that many non-Japanese also have — one that looks first to the present environment and the people in it. Other frequent solutions to the problem are:

I'd look at my watch to see how much time I had.

I would just sit and think about it for a few moments.

I wouldn't have a problem; I always allow extra time for emergencies.

I don't know exactly what I'd do, but I know I'd keep that appointment somehow, if it was really important (to me).

I would think, 'Oh God, this isn't my day', and go back to bed.

Remember that most people, in such a dilemma, would probably combine a number of linked and related strategies. They would check how much time they had, check the car quickly for small, easily reparable faults, make a telephone call about the appointment, find other forms of transport, get the car towed away, and so on. In other words, everybody can use experience, reflective observation, abstract theorization, and practical action to solve problems. Games like 'My Car Won't Start' are useful only if you and the players do not try to generalize too much from limited data. However, the results may suggest that perhaps you are likely to be working, say, with a group of people who are planners rather than doers — they might be insurance company actuaries, for example. Games like those described above can give you some ideas for presenting your material attractively to learners of this type in order to motivate them to learn more effectively.

You can also learn a lot about your learners by asking them to solve little puzzles — of mathematics or logic — but the puzzles have to be chosen carefully. There are any number available — you can buy books of them at any newsagent or bookstore — but just any old puzzle will not do; it has to be one which contains the kind of ambiguity that will start people arguing about the solution. In other words, puzzles as games for learning have to provoke conflict.

The following are five examples. They are all quite different from each other, yet they have in common this element of surprise, or controversy. For instance, the first one, 'A to B' is an exercise in abstract, logical thinking. There is no real trick to it, though many players will argue with you that there is. It is one of the best exercises that we know for demonstrating experientially some differences between people's perceptions of a problem and the resulting differences in the method of solving it. Allow at least half an hour and be prepared for a lot of conflict, often heated.

'A to B'

Give the class this problem:

> 'I travel from A to B at an average speed of 20 miles per hour. Without stopping or deviating from my route in any way I return to A. At what speed will I have to complete the return journey in order to average 40 miles per hour for the *round trip?*'

Most people average the speeds and calculate that the return journey must be made at 60 miles per hour $(20+60=80$ divided by $2=40)$. In fact the answer is infinity (in other words, it cannot be done) because nothing can alter the fact that the traveller is being asked to complete a distance in the same time he or she has already taken to cover only half of it.

Generally speaking, people who are temperamentally well suited to abstract problem-solving — who enjoy puzzles for their own sake — are likely to arrive first at the right answer because they have worked it out logically, one bit at a time, and deductively, ie by a process of convergent reasoning; and therefore they will also be able to explain why. Sometimes they will respond apparently intuitively with the correct answer without knowing why.

Problem-solvers of the latter variety appear to take a holistic view of a given situation. It is as if they become sensitive to the 'feel' of it and then come up with a solution that 'seems right' or 'sounds right'. Instead of breaking the problem up into a logical sequence their reasoning is non-logical and inductive; they make the problem bigger, and allow a number of possible solutions to converge on to it.

Neither of these primarily abstract problem-solvers seems to be particularly worried if they happen to get the answer wrong; they do not have a great deal of emotional capital invested in the outcome. On the face of it this seems a ridiculous thing to say, because why should anybody be upset if they do not get the right answer to a silly little guessing game? Nevertheless, 'A to B' makes a lot of people cross — which is one of the things that makes it a good game — because they have based their answer on their own life experience. They know from experience that in real life if they are running late they can run faster and catch up.

You can explain until you are blue in the face that they cannot drive 40 miles in one hour if they have already driven for an hour and covered only half the distance. You can prove it by assuming the same average speeds over any distance; but they will not believe you. One woman became so angry that we were thankful to call a temporary halt for lunch, with the promise to clear the matter up afterwards. She was the only person in the class who had continued to reject the right answer and we could not get on with the course until she was satisfied. We were dreading the afternoon session, but, when it began, the woman nobly asked if she could stand up in front of the whole class. This is what she said.

> 'I didn't eat any lunch. I've spent the past hour with a pencil and paper, working out this wretched problem by assuming a number of different distances for the journey; and I can't do it. I realize now that no matter what the distance, the journey can't be done. I still don't know why, but I want to tell everybody that I'm sorry I was so rude, and that I accept their answer.'

She became much happier when one of the group members offered the comment that the answer to 'A to B' lies in the relationship between the two average speeds; and that if the traveller were to be allowed a lower overall average speed, say 30 instead of 40 mph, the traveller could indeed do — at least in theory — what the woman suggested, ie drive faster on the return journey and increase the overall average speed from 20 to 30 mph. The woman was able to say: 'I knew it was a trick!', which left her self-esteem relatively undamaged. People who are fundamentally more concerned with human experience than facts and figures tend to put a low value on numeracy. Hence, their self-respect is undamaged if the solution to a problem is shown to be 'only a matter of figures'.

Now for another example that requires logical thinking.

'Ships of the Line'

Many years ago, at 12.00 noon daily, a ship from the P & O line used to leave Honolulu for Sydney. The journey used to take seven days.

Also in those days, at 12.00 noon daily, a P & O ship used to leave Sydney for Honolulu. The course was the same, the journey also took seven days, and all times were GMT. Once I boarded one of these ships at Honolulu, bound for Sydney. How many P & O ships did I see on my journey?

It really does not matter what the 'right' answer is to this problem, because in attempting to solve it the discussion will range far and wide, to cover the International Date Line; whether the traveller is standing on the port or starboard side of the ship, and so on. We have found it an advantage sometimes not to know the answer to a puzzle. It puts all the onus of responsibility on the students. After a moment or two of outrage that they have been offered a puzzle without a short-cut to the answer (ie by waiting passively for the 'teacher' to tell them), a few people will start tackling the problem in real earnest and come up with a solution that everybody can usually be persuaded to accept — which is a good example of leadership style.

Now for something a bit more dramatic.

'Harry's Dog'

Harry had a small, fluffy dog of which he was very fond. Unfortunately his girlfriend liked the dog too. When she offered to buy it from Harry for £10, which was all she could afford, he felt that she had to have it. However, he missed the animal so badly that he gave his girlfriend £20 the next day and took the dog home. His friend, whose name was Mary, still wanted the dog, so she saved up another £10 and offered Harry £30. Poor Harry did not like to refuse so he let her have the dog and took the £30. But by this time he was feeling fed up with the whole business, so after a couple of days he went to see Mary, gave her £40, and asked for his dog; which is the end of the story. The questions are, did anybody finally make a profit out of these transactions, and, if so, who and what? And then you ask people to write their answers down and not show them to anybody yet.

When they have had a few moments to think about it, ask people at random to read out what they have written, and you will find that others volunteer their answers as soon as they realize how differently they have perceived the problem.

Some people will reply that Mary made a profit of £20, which is the right answer if the question is interpreted as a simple matter of economics, of profit and loss. They add up the total income and outgoings of one of the characters and subtract one from the other — for example, Mary's income was £60 and her expenditure was £40. Therefore, since she made a profit of £20, Harry incurred a loss of the same amount. (Some people have difficulty with this transition and you may have to post the income and expenditure of both characters. This is a good warm-up to a mathematics class for young students or an elementary course in budgeting, etc.)

Some people will get the answer wrong, but that is because they have made a mistake in their arithmetic, not because they have perceived the problem differently from those who got it right. However, there are usually some others in the group who have been motivated to find answers that are different in kind.

They will reply that Harry's profit was that he kept the dog, or that his loss was that he lost his girlfriend, or that the girlfriend was the greater loser because she lost both the dog and — they presume — Harry, or that everybody won because it could reasonably be assumed that Harry, Mary and the dog moved in together, or that the dog was the ultimate loser because it had a nervous breakdown.

You will find a much plainer version of this game, called 'John's Dog', in Pfeiffer and Jones (1975). If you play it according to their instructions, you are much less likely to get the rich range of response that we have described above. This is an example of how you can take a very basic activity like a straightforward mathematical puzzle and dress it up dramatically to provide a real learning experience for the participants. Here is another one.

'The Shoe Saleswoman'

A customer goes into a shoe shop and buys a pair of shoes that have been marked down in a sale to £12. He pays for the shoes with a £20 note. The sales assistant does not have change at that early hour of the morning, so she asks him to wait, and runs next door to the Italian greengrocer, who exchanges the note for smaller notes. The assistant then returns to her customer and gives him £8 change; he leaves the store with the shoes. Later in the day, the greengrocer comes to see her, very upset. He has spotted the £20 as a counterfeit, and has informed the police, who will visit her shortly. The poor woman feels very bad about this, apologizes to the greengrocer for all the trouble she has unwittingly caused, takes £20 out of her till to reimburse him, and prepares herself for the arrival of the police.

The question is, how much actual cash (we are not talking about the stock value of the shoes) is she out of pocket now? The answer is £8, because the counterfeit bill was only a worthless piece of paper and does not count. All that matters is that she received £20 from the greengrocer which she returned later, so that transaction cancels itself out; therefore, all she has lost is the £8 change she gave the customer.

When you dramatize these puzzles in the telling, you increase the likelihood that some players will act out the problem physically in order to 'see' the answer for themselves. Thus in 'Harry's Dog' it is quite possible that some people will say to each other: 'Here, you be Harry, I'll be Mary, and you be the dog!' Then the dog will trot meekly from one to the other, while they solemnly exchange torn-up pieces of paper for money; then when the play is over, they count the pieces to find out who has got more. With 'The Shoe Saleswoman' some people will use 'real' money, in the form of paper, to work it out. In fact, we have known people to use their own money from their wallets, laying it out on the tale in front of them and apportioning the various sums to designated players.

When this happens, you have a highly visible illustration of some of the differences between experiential and abstract problem-solving styles, and you can point to the advantages and disadvantages of both: for example, that dramatization is slower, if you are looking for a particular kind of answer — ie mathematical — but richer if you are looking at human behaviour and personal interaction.

Another game that can stimulate players' imaginations is 'The princess and the Peasant'.

'The Princess and the Peasant'

A peasant wanted to marry a princess. Her father, the king, was furious and ordered that the peasant should have his head cut off for impertinence. But the peasant was handsome, and the queen was sentimental and wanted her daughter to be happy; so she persuaded the King to give the peasant a sporting chance. It was agreed that he should draw one of two cards out of a box and accept what was written on it as his fate. One card would say 'marriage' and the other 'death'. However, the king cheated and marked both cards 'death', and put them in the box. The queen saw him do it and rushed off to tell the princess, who was able to get word to her lover. When the time came to draw the card, the peasant did so, and bore the consequences — which were that he married the princess and lived happily ever after. How did he do it?

A possible answer is that he drew a card and without looking at it, tore it up and said: 'Let the King draw the other card so that I may learn my fate at his hands. If he draws "marriage" I will know my card was "death" and will accept my fate.'

This puzzle is best written down, with a copy given to each of the participants. Let them read it and think about it; and then get into sub-groups to discuss it if the class is large. It is a good warm-up, as it gets people talking in a light-hearted atmosphere that stimulates lateral thinking.

The following is an example of a different kind of imagination game.

'Think of a Cube'

Ask everybody to sit in a comfortable and relaxed position. You can do a short relaxation exercise first, if you think the group will benefit from it, such as deep breathing or bending and stretching. When everybody is quiet and still, you assume the mantle of a storyteller and say, with suitable emphases and pauses:

> 'Imagine a cube . . . whatever comes into your mind that is in the shape of a cube . . . now separate the cube into two . . . now separate each of the two pieces of your cube into two . . . now get rid of them and see what you're left with.'

Did you picture a real or an abstract cube (eg a piece of sugar or a shape in the space)? Do you know what it looked like, felt like, tasted like? What colour was it? How big was it? Where was it? Was the setting clearly defined? Were you there with the cube, wherever it was? Was anybody else there?

The next set of questions relate to dividing the cube:

> Did you divide it or did it divide itself? Did anybody help you? Did you use a tool? Did you hear anything? Did you get your hands dirty or sticky? Did it divide cleanly or was there a mess? Were the two pieces equal in size? When there were four pieces, were they all cubes? Were they all alike? Were they very small?

Then ask how people made their cubes disappear:

> How did you get rid of it? Did it just disappear, like an animated cartoon? Did you eat it? Throw it away? Give it away? Wish it away?

As you ask these questions, people's imaginations will begin to stretch and they will improvise details. We remember a woman describing in minute detail how in her mind she was in her kitchen and there was a lump of sugar in front of her on the wooden chopping block. She went to cut it with a knife but she cut her finger and got distracted by the blood, a drop of which fell on to the sugar. She became fascinated by the contrast of red on white. When she had to cut the sugar again, she tried to cut it in such a way that there was a tiny speck of blood on each piece. There were too many for her to count — lots and lots of tiny cubes of sugar all over the block, all touched with one drop of blood. She did not know how to get rid of them all; the vision had become stressful. She found herself thinking, 'If I don't get rid of them, if I just walk out, I shall be frightened to go back into the kitchen'. So she shovelled them all up with her hands into a plastic garbage bag and then tipped them out into the garden for the birds to eat.

It seems odd at first, perhaps, that this woman should report, as she did, that she had thoroughly enjoyed the experience. It may be that adults are not given enough opportunity in everday life to exercise their imagination and that a game like 'Think of a Cube' fills a gap. However, when you get feedback as strong as this from a warm-up or trigger game, you know you have got at least one participant in your group whose imagination will run way ahead of you. That is great, but if her learning style is not balanced by the styles of other participants who are more theoretical or abstract in their responses, you will have to make those responses yourself. With luck, you will find some players who have dreamed up cubes that are shapes in the air, that divide themselves like computer graphics, that vanish without fuss and without trace. Note also that some people are more visual than others, while others are more sound-oriented. (Some participants in 'Think of a Cube' will tell you that they heard it break; others will express astonishment at this concept.)

These kinds of feedback will help you to structure group discussions so that the participants hear more than one viewpoint. This will enable students to develop a multi-dimensional view of a problem and its solution, rather than one subject to the constraints of 'one right answer'. This multi-dimensional view of problem-solving must be developed if you are to negotiate with them the meanings of the material you have contracted to 'teach' them. This is the objective for which you design your games.

Chapter 3

Games for Young Players

Over the years we have been asked to design and evaluate many educational games for younger players, and we have come to the conclusion that while most youngsters enjoy these activities, they do not always appear to learn a great deal from them. However, this result may be more the responsibility of the game director than the game. We have come to this conclusion because some primary school teachers and youth workers do not seem to have this problem when they use games as learning strategies. This may mean that those of us who are accustomed to working with adults should acquire slightly different leadership skills when we are with younger students.

People learn from games from the inside out. First they experience a number of feelings when they play a game, then they are encouraged by the game director to use inductive reasoning to relate these feelings, as well as their observations of other players' behaviour, to wider, more general and theoretical contexts. Some educators argue that children are not as capable of this process as are adults. For example, Malcolm Knowles (1977) suggests that experience-based learning methods are more appropriate for adults than for children because the former have a much wider framework of knowledge and experience within which to locate their responses.

We have some doubts about this line of argument because from earliest infancy (and even earlier, according to some theorists), children begin the experiential learning cycle. Long before they can talk they are capable of reflecting on their experiences and generalizing from them to experiment actively with new behaviour. A simple example is the way babies learn to recognize that a bottle-shaped or cup-shaped object means 'drink', and the way they start to yell every time they see such a thing — only to learn soon enough that they do not always get a drink in return; so they modify their behaviour accordingly.

By the time children start school, they have built up reserves of life experience that in some respects may be deeper than those of their teachers. For example, they may have already learned survival tactics in a harder school than anything the Department of Education can provide. Nevertheless, children and young teenagers do seem to experience a certain amount of difficulty in thinking of games as analogous to real life, partly because they are socialized under most educational systems to think that games are fun and learning is not.

Also we have a theory that many groups of young people will not be able to realize a game's potential unless the game director takes into account three characteristics such groups frequently possess:

(1) A short concentration span.
(2) A high level of free-floating aggression.
(3) Low motivation.

Acting on these assumptions, the following are some of the games we designed or adapted for groups of youngsters of various ages from about 12 to 18 years old. Built into these game structures are features that seem to increase players' concentration, release their aggression in constructive ways, and motivate them at least to see some advantages and possibilities in trying to take more control of their own lives.

The first one is a short 'test'; we did not invent this game and have no idea where it came from originally, but we like it because it always seems to provoke animated discussion. Students have to complete many tests, but the sting in the tail of 'Test with a Moral' seems to stimulate respondents' critical abilities. Therefore, we hope it helps them to be less passive as learners. We think it is also a good prelude to other activities that encourage young students to think about the concepts of planning ahead and time-management of tasks in general.

'Test with a Moral'

Can you follow directions? Try this timed test, allowing yourself three minutes only.
   (1) Read everything carefully before doing anything.
   (2) Print your name in the upper right-hand corner of this paper.
   (3) Circle your name.
   (4) Draw five small squares in the upper left-hand corner of this paper.
   (5) Put an 'X' in each square.
   (6) Sign your name at the top of this paper.
   (7) Under your name in the upper right-hand corner, write your telephone number. If you do not have one, write the number 100.
   (8) Call out loudly the number you have written, so that everybody can hear you.

(9) Circle this number

(10) Put an 'X' in the lower left-hand corner of this paper.

(11) Draw a triangle round it.

(12) Count out loud in your normal speaking voice, from 10 to 1 backwards.

(13) Draw a rectangle around the word 'corner' in sentence number 4.

(14) Punch three small holes in the top of this paper, with your pencil or pen point.

(15) Call out loud: 'I am nearly finished'.

(16) Now that you have finished reading everything carefully, do only sentences 1 and 2.

We are sorry to have to report that most of the groups to whom we have administered this test get at least halfway down the list, and usually further, before they become at all suspicious. The majority of players aged around 11 to 13 take it all quite seriously. They assume that the questions are designed to test their ability to follow instructions, to write and draw neatly, and to recognize simple geometric terms like 'triangle'. The test does not strike them, at first, as being very different from many 'class tests' they have had to endure in the past — which we think is an indictment of such tests.

Some students complain that they have been 'tricked' when they complete 'Test with a Moral' without reading it first, and some are glad that they did not read it because they enjoyed doing all the tasks, which they found relaxing in a pleasantly mindless way. It is a good warm-up game because it sharpens players' concentration and increases their motivation for the next exercise. If you follow it up with a planning game, such as 'Picnic' (below), you may be able to initiate a thoughtful discussion about the advantages of planning one's work instead of pitching in and doing the first thing that apparently needs doing. The discussion can possibly be expanded to include subjects like planning one's homework, organizing essay writing, balancing work and leisure, and so on; but the group's motivation may fall off sharply if you introduce these subjects too crudely, because the participants may feel very negative about them.

'Picnic'

This game is called 'Picnic' because in its original form, which we still use occasionally, players in groups of three to five people are asked to plan a picnic at a local but isolated beauty spot, using only their own resources or those they know they can call upon. Then the groups are asked to compare notes and discuss the items they have included and to think of others they might have overlooked — insect repellent, a book to read, the transport they will need. Finally we announce that the overall plan sounds so reasonable that the picnic will actually take place, and name the date.

We have since discovered with other groups of young people that 'Picnic' can be adapted to suit their particular needs; even though we have never changed the name, nobody ever seems to find it inappropriate. For example, we asked a group of adolescent boys on a rehabilitation course (they had all been in trouble with the police for crimes such as theft) to play 'Picnic' by assuming the roles of police officers who plan to stake out a house which they have reason to believe will be robbed. The boys entered into the spirit of the exercise so efficiently that we agreed with them on a simple scenario and asked them if they would like to act out their plan. The result was an amazing role-play in which the 'police' engaged the 'villains' so realistically in physical combat that we really thought for a few moments that we had lost control of the whole situation and would have to summon outside help. However, the players had the matter in hand and no real damage was done to persons or property — though several 'cops' kicked a door so vigorously (to get at the 'robbers') that the paintwork suffered. Their enactment of police violence was so graphic that we asked the group afterwards to discuss this aspect of the game, and gained some useful insights of the views that the boys had of law enforcement methods in general.

We put all our cards on the table when we debriefed the game. We pointed out to these players that they certainly did not lack planning skills — the simulation was planned and executed very competently — and that they were capable of high levels of concentration. We drew to their attention the fact that the choice of subject for the role-play had given them the motivation they needed to display these abilities, and had also provided them with an opportunity to release some of their pent-up anger, frustration and hostility in physical activity. We ended by suggesting that the mere fact of our drawing these things to their attention might give them food for thought about ways in which they might apply their undoubted abilities to planning their futures — in other words, to self-leadership — and left it at that.

'Grapevine'

This game is useful for studying communications systems in organizations. It demonstrates flow-patterns of communication, and where delays and bottlenecks can build up. However, we do not describe it in these words when we introduce it to groups of young players. We introduce it as a game to show, for example, how a class of students can increase their learning capacity, and their pleasure in learning, by exchanging information effectively.

You will need a stopwatch, a pack of playing cards, a pen or pencil for each player, and masses of paper for them to write on. You can cut up sheets of paper into smaller squares to prevent waste. You will also need adhesive labels to stick on players' foreheads, stating whether they are A, B, C, D, E or R (which stands for Runner).

'Grapevine' is played in two rounds, with teams of six people. It is a competitive game, so you will need at least 12 players, and if there are any observers left over, so much the better. They can change places with team-members in Round 2.

For Round 1, put each team into a circle. All the circles should be as large as possible, so use the whole space of the room. Each circle consists of five team-members, preferably sitting on the floor, each person facing outwards from the circle. The sixth member of each team stands or sits in the middle of his or her circle.

Label the foreheads of the people in each circle A, B, C, D and E, respectively. Give these sets of five people a playing card per person and ask them not to let anybody else see what it is. The sixth person in each circle, the one in the middle, is labelled R. These players are the Runners who have to run messages for their respective teams.

The object of the game is that every player must complete a list naming the card each person in the circle holds. The rules are that no talking is allowed; the information has to be shared by written notes, which are carried by the Runner. Everybody in any one circle can communicate with their Runner, and with the person on either side of them in the circle. Thus A can communicate with B and E; B with A and C; C with B and D; D with C and E; and E with D and A.

For example, player A may write a note addressed to B, asking: 'What card is C holding?' A then raises his or her hand, the Runner comes over, checks that there is only one question on the note, then takes and delivers it to B. As soon as team-members have received the replies that they need to complete their lists, they stand up (though they can continue to receive and send notes from and to their neighbours who have not yet finished). When all of the team-members in a circle are standing, the Runner collects the five lists and takes them to the game director, who has been timing the round with a stopwatch. The winner is the team whose runner is the first to reach the game leader with the five complete and correct lists.

If any team-member talks, the team is penalized by having 30 seconds added to its time. If a team-member is caught cheating by showing his or her card to another player or players, the team is disqualified. When Round 1 is over, Round 2 begins. The players are labelled and seated in circles as for Round 1. The objective is the same — ie all five team-members shall know what card each of them holds — but now team-members can communicate only with the Runner and one other player in the circle (we usually designate C to be this person, for no real reason). Again the players can send only one note and one question at a time, but now all their questions are directed to C. They raise their hands when they want the Runner, and stand up when they have received enough information from C to inform them of the card each of their four team-mates holds.

Theoretically, the time taken to complete Round 1 should be shorter than for Round 2, because in Round 1 more people can communicate with each other directly, and in practice this is usually the case. However, several factors can complicate the issue and Round 2 is frequently shorter — for example, if the sole information-disseminator (player C) is quick and accurate, the Runner is fast, and the other four players have organized their questions effectively and have their notes ready for the runner. Also they have the advantage that they have already played Round 1, so if they are quick learners their working speed will have increased. These are all observations that you can share with the players when the game is over; you can also help them to relate these observations to the basics of organizational (ie group) communication.

'Grapevine' often has the effect of increasing group cohesiveness in a class of school students, and individuals' sense of commitment to their classmates as a team. The game leader can enhance young students' sense of self-worth and encourage them to think about the uniqueness of their contribution to the group by drawing real-life parallels with the game — the ability of one person to collate information from a number of sources, for instance, or the speed and accuracy of another.

Our next game is of a very different order. It takes a week to play and students find it a deeply emotional experience, so beware!

'The Egg Adoption Project'

We have adapted this game from an original by Dave Wheeler, who ran it as a student assignment for a course in Child Care General Studies in Australia. We have also heard of it being played in a guidance class with 16 to 17-year-olds in a private school in Honolulu, which makes it an international exercise.

The scenario is that each student in the group adopts one raw egg and keeps it safe and well for one whole week. The 'parents' have to keep a daily diary describing their experiences, itemize and account for any financial outgoings in connection with the adopted egg, and complete a questionnaire at the end of the experience.

If you are engaged in community work with young people, particularly disadvantaged young people with family problems, or if you are in charge of a class of young students, or are otherwise in a situation where you can use this game, it will give you and your group some insights about parent-child relationships.

Give each youngster a raw egg at the beginning of the week, with the following instructions. The egg must be kept in good health — neither too warm nor too cold — and given plenty of fresh air, sunshine, and exercise in safe surroundings where it cannot be damaged. It must be kept neat and clean with regular washing and must not be deprived of human companionship. Either the 'parent' or a competent surrogate must be with it at all times during its waking hours, and it must have access at reasonable intervals to a stimulating environment. It must be talked to, and taken on outings. It can be carried in a pocket, providing it has enough air and its comfort is checked regularly. While the 'parent' is sleeping, the egg should be kept close by, preferably within sight. If the responsibilities of 'parenthood' become too great, the 'parent' may hire an egg-sitter for 50 pence an hour and this expense must be noted in the diary. (Dave Wheeler's suggestion is that at the end of the week all such money should be collected and donated to the Royal Society for the Blind, to assist blind babies.) If disaster should occur and an egg be lost or broken, the 'parent' must pay the funeral costs of £2 and observe a period of mourning of not less than two days. After this period another egg may be obtained.

The questionnaire asks the name and age of the 'parent' and — to be answered at the end of the week — such questions as:

- Which period in the week was the most difficult and why? Which was the easiest and why?
- How did other people react to your becoming an egg parent? Why do you think they reacted this way?
- How many hours during the week did you spend with your egg in your physical possession? With your egg outdoors? Without your egg in your care?
- What was the total cost incurred by you on behalf of your egg?
- Did your feelings about your egg change during the week? Describe any such change.
- Has this exercise altered your feelings about the responsibilities of parenthood? What similarities do you think there are between the demands made on you to care for your egg and the responsibilities of having a real child?
- What additional demands would a child make on you?
- Are there any further comments you would like to add?

We stress, as we have before, that teaching is a form of persuasion. It may be, for example, that you are in a counselling situation where you want to use 'The Egg Adoption Project' to emphasize some of the problems and commitments involved in becoming an unmarried teenage parent. In that case, you may want to add a few questions to the above list. Examples of more potentially value-laden questions might be:

● What rewards did you find in caring for your egg?
● At what age do you think you would like to start your family, and how many children do you think you would like to have?

Anecdotes about 'The Egg Adoption Project' include those of 'parents' who painted faces on their eggs, gave them names, took them into the shower with them, made clothes for them, and bought them toys. There is the story of the parent who broke her egg and was too upset to go to school for two days; and the tale of the egg 'father' who made his real-life sister take care of his egg because he said it was more her job than his — even though his little sister had nothing to do with the project. Both boys and girls have reported that by about the fifth day of the experiment, they became really 'irritated' by the responsibility of caring for their eggs. It ceased to be fun and became a burden, even though the actual work was slight.

Egg 'mothers' sometimes report their fear of becoming too attached to their eggs; in consequence, they made conscious decisions to view the whole experiment very pragmatically. In this connection, it is interesting to note that a leading American pediatrician, Dr Berry Brazelton, suggests that when mothers know that they will have to separate early from their infants because they have to return to work, they deliberately withold emotion from the child; therefore a necessary bonding process is not completed and the child may suffer permanent emotional damage which can affect all of his or her later relationships. This is an interesting idea to discuss with participants in 'The Egg Adoption Project'. The position of married women in the workforce is constantly under threat in industrialized societies, particularly in times of economic recession; and when members of the medical profession join the fray with arguments such as those of Dr Brazelton, these arguments have to be evaluated within a socio-political context. Thus games such as 'The Egg Adoption Project' can help participants — particularly girls — to become more aware of social pressures.

The next game is called 'Gene Scene' and we designed it for science teachers. This and the following games are intended primarily for school students who have problems with absorbing and retaining information of a fairly abstract and theoretical nature, when it is presented to them by a traditional teaching method. Such students — who can become quite recalcitrant through sheer frustration — are often very much encouraged when they discover that a different teaching style can improve their motivation and concentration. This realization takes some of the pressure off them to 'perform' as model pupils and puts part of the responsibility for their learning on to their teachers to 'deliver the goods' in ways these students can relate to and learn from.

'Gene Scene' aims to illustrate some aspects of human genetic inheritance. Mendel seems to have been somewhat discredited by modern geneticists, and we hope that the format of this game will not suggest that we are out-of-date old fogeys. The last time we played 'Gene Scene' with a group of science teachers was in 1983, when it was well received, but if you disagree with our suggested charts below, you can always make others. Such changes will not affect the general objectives of the game, which are:

— To demonstrate the chance factor in genetic inheritance.
— To suggest the twin notions of dominant and recessive genes and some possible results of their combinations.
— To indicate some degree of inevitability in the inheritance of certain individual physical characteristics.
— To illustrate the discreteness of some genetic characteristics.
— To provide facility in working out some possible genetic combinations, which includes practice in elementary mathematical skills.

'Gene Scene'

You need to be either a science teacher with from eight to about 40 students, aged about 13 years, or a science teacher-trainer who wants to play this game with adult students. The ideal number is probably somewhere from 16 to 24 and the game will run over two class periods, ie something under two hours. It is not a good idea to play it in two separate class periods with other lessons in between.

The room must be large enough for the players to move around freely, preferably unimpeded by tables or desks, which should be either absent completely or pushed back against the walls. You need a clear space in the middle to set up as many chairs as there are players, less two. The chairs are arranged as for the game of 'Musical Chairs', ie in a line down the middle of the room, the chairs alternately facing one way and then the other. You will also need a board or wall on which to display charts, and sticky labels that will adhere to players' clothing or foreheads. The players will all need writing materials, and you will need to provide a cassette player and a tape of any music with a good, strong beat. (Adolescents have strong likes and dislikes about music — and everything else — so you could enquire in advance of the group or the regular teacher, whether one of the players would be willing to bring in a cassette of the latest popular favourite.)

Divide the players into two groups, those with blue eyes and those with brown. If most of the players have blue eyes, or brown, because of a shared ethnic background, divide them into groups of people who respectively can and cannot roll their tongues; or those who have curly hair and those whose hair is straight. Other possible genetic characteristics for 'Gene Scene' players include the possession or not of earlobes , or the respective length of their toes.

Give each person a sticky label and ask them to indicate their genetic inheritance by following the instructions on the charts you have prepared in advance and now post. Our examples (Figures 1 and 2) refer to blue and brown eyes.

The eye colour brown is from a dominant gene; the eye colour blue is from a recessive gene. You have inherited 50 per cent of your genes (half of them) from your mother and 50 per cent from your father. If you have blue eyes, this is because your inherited genes for eye colour are blue. Therefore write bb on your label (b = blue). If you have brown eyes, at least one of your inherited genes for eye colour must be brown. Your symbol, therefore, will be either BB (B = brown) or bB. You do not know which it is, but for the purpose of the game you can choose to write either. When you have written either bb or BB or bB on your label in large letters, stick it on to your forehead so everybody can see it.

Figure 1. *Gene Chart*

This diagram shows what might happen when six couples, with various combinations of eye colour between them, each have four children:

— bb and bb will produce: bb, bb, bb and bb (all children will have blue eyes)
— bb and bB will produce: bb, bB, bb and Bb (any of their children will have a 50 per cent chance of blue or brown eyes)
— bb and BB will produce: bB, Bb, Bb, and Bb (all children will have brown eys)
— BB and BB will produce: BB, BB, BB and BB (all children will have brown eyes)
— bB and BB will produce: bB, bB, BB and BB (all children will have brown eyes)
— bB and bB will produce: bb, bB, bB and BB (any child has a 25 per cent chance of blue eyes and a 75 per cent chance of brown eyes).

If A is blue-eyed and Z is brown-eyed and they have 12 children, the following are the possible combinations of eye colour for their children:

There will be a 25 per cent chance of any child having blue eyes and a 75 per cent chance of any child having brown eyes: that is:

bb + bB (or BB) will produce: bb, bB, bb, bB, bb, bB, bB, bB, bB, bB, bB, bB.

Figure 2. *Blue eyes = bb. Brown eyes = BB or bB.*

Now set up a game of Musical Chairs, which you announce as Musical Genes. All participants move round the line of chairs in time to the music and when you stop it they have to sit down on the nearest empty chair. There is always a certain amount of pushing and shoving at this point, which is all to the good. One of the reasons for the success of this game is that it alternates bursts of noisy physical group activity with short periods of concentration.

Two people will be left without chairs; they stand in front of the line and become the focus of a brief discussion in which you ask a couple of questions, for example, 'Jane, you have very blue eyes; are both your parents blue-eyed?' It is perhaps worth noting at this point that if you have a group of players whose general motivation is very low, Jane might very likely respond perversely — perhaps something to the effect of, 'Don't know, I haven't seen my Dad since I was little'; or 'No, my Dad's got brown eyes', which puts you in the position of having to probe further to check whether perhaps her 'Dad' is, in fact, her stepfather.

Enhancement of self-worth in the players is always an important aspect of gaming; therefore, answer this kind of obstructionism with an acknowledgement of Jane's unique individuality (a sense of which she may well have been expressing indirectly by her attitude, though she may not have been able fully to articulate it even to herself). Perhaps you could say something about everybody being unique, and rightly proud of it, but that it is fun to find out a bit more about the ways in which such uniqueness came about.

If the couple are a boy and a girl, you can discuss the possibility of their getting married, in which case what would be the chances of any one of their children having blue or brown eyes? You have to be careful how you 'marry people off' in some groups, as you may have to put up with a lot of crude mirth. With more sophisticated groups, or older players (which is not always the same thing) you can introduce a second genetic characteristic, such as the ability to roll one's tongue; but be warned, this complicates the discussion to a surprising extent.

When you have exhausted the possibilities of this pair of players, ask them to help you remove two chairs from the line and restart the music for the next round of the game. Let the remaining players race around the chairs for a few moments before stopping the music to get yourself another pair of blue or brown-eyed players, and so on. When the game is over you can initiate, if you want, some kind of discussion about topics like race prejudice, based on the colour of people's eyes or skin or the shape of their noses. Alternatively (or as well), you can include a short exercise in another kind of self-validation. Introduce the question of how much of an individual's total personality is derived from his or her parents and how much is due to other factors, such as life experience, environment, the influence of friends and teachers, and so on. Ask all of the players to draw a circle which represents themselves, then a circle which represents their mother, intersecting with their own circle in any way they like — or even not at all; then a third circle, to represent their father, which also intersects with their personal circle in any way they think appropriate, or not at all (and they may choose to intersect the circles representing their mother and father as well); the drawing should represent what they feel about their own identity within this three-way relationship. Then ask for volunteers to share with the group their reasons for drawing their circles the way they did. We hope we do not need to stress the importance of your remaining non-judgmental throughout this activity.

Now for another game suitable for a biology or natural science class. It aims to illustrate the process of digestion in the human body, but it also provides opportunity for its young players to work as a team towards a common task — which offers motivation and demands concentration.

'Down it Goes!'

This can be played with any very large groups of students, with a minimum of about 20. The game takes about 50 minutes, including discussion. You will have prepared in advance the following chart, which you post at the beginning of the game.

Food is:
● Chewed;
● Passed down a long coil of gut;
● Mixed with enzymes;
● Enzymes break up food;
● Food is moved along by muscle action;
● Soluble food is absorbed into walls of small intestine;
● Is taken by blood to liver and stored;
● Is taken by blood to other cells for energy;
● Insoluble food is passed through large intestine and out of anus;
● Energy is released.

You may like to do a warm-up with the group before you start 'Down it Goes!', as the 'body machine' the players are going to build will demand close cooperation between its living parts. For example, you could ask the players to stand in a close circle (or several circles if group numbers are large) and then ask a volunteer to stand in the middle, close his or her eyes, fall backwards and allow him or herself to be caught by members of the circle. Curiously enough, in view of the temperament of some of the young people we have worked with, we have never known anybody to get hurt during this warm-up. Nobody in our experience has ever been allowed by the circle to fall to the ground, though they have not always been handled very gently in the process of being saved. If you have any doubts at all, remind yourself that if you were not a risk-taker you would not be a game leader, stand yourself in the middle of the circle, shut your eyes, and fall backwards. We felt it necessary to do this once, and we are still alive and well enough to report that our action 'gentled' the group to a remarkable extent.

When you feel ready to begin 'Down it Goes!' divide the players into groups of at least 20 people each. Tell everybody that they are going to build a body machine that will simulate the process of digestion in the human body, and assign the following roles to individual players:

- Fresh air (one or more roles, depending on numbers);
- Food (four roles);
- Jaws (two roles);
- Gut (at least five roles);
- Enzymes (two roles);
- Enzymes with villae, ie waving, whisker-like hairs (two roles);
- The division between the large and small intestine (one role);
- The liver (one role);
- The anus (two roles).

If you have more players than you need, the remainder can form more 'gut' or they may prefer to stay outside the body machine in the 'fresh air'. What has to happen is this: two lines of players stand opposite each other, with a passageway between them, blocked in the middle by the 'division between the large and small intestine'. This 'body machine' represents the parts of the human body that are concerned with the process of digestion, and the lane between them represents in turn the jaws, the alimentary canal, the large and small intestine, the liver and the anus. The passageway is narrow to start with, but broadens out like an upside-down Y after the division between large and small intestine.

Jaw................Jaw
Gut................Gut
Gut................Gut
Enzyme............Enzyme
Division

Villae.....................................Villae
(digested food will join line here)................(and here)

Liver.....................................Gut
Anus ....Anus

The player who represents 'fresh air' walks or runs round the body while digestion takes place. Now the four 'mouthfuls of food', one after the other, enter the passage between the 'jaws', who push them (gently!) into two pairs, and on into the 'alimentary canal'. The four players who line the canal as part of the 'gut' continue this rhythmic pushing action until the two pairs of 'food pieces' reach the 'enzymes', who separate the pairs into single units. This brings the food pieces, one at a time, to the 'division between the large and small intestine'. The player who represents the 'division' pushes the four food pieces into position as follows:

- Two of them are passed right down the passage and out through 'the anus', where they join the 'fresh air'.
- The other two merge into the 'gut wall' of the 'small intestine', where the 'villae' extend their arms to receive them (one ends up standing beside a 'gut' player in the line and the other beside the 'liver' — see the above diagram).

In real life, when digested food and air meet in the bloodstream, energy is released. Therefore, when all the food particles have been assigned to their proper places, the whole body machine starts to jump up and down and shout. This whole sequence of events is quite complicated; it has to be worked out first in slow motion with explanations and discussions at each stage of construction of the body machine. Construction will take about an hour, and then a couple of practice runs are needed until all the parts of the machine understand what they have to do. If the final performance is sufficiently synchronized, it can be performed to music, but we cannot guarantee that you will get that far with your group. However, it is an excellent learning excercise, not only for its content but also for the encouragement it gives players to work together in harmony. They are able to see themselves as individuals, each of whom plays a unique and vital role in a problem-solving exercise that demands concentration but provides a stimulating activity that justifies the effort. The players always seem to find it both informative and fun, though many students are quite slow to 'catch on' to the concept of using people to make a living model. 'Down it Goes!' is also a useful exercise for trainee teachers, both as an example of a learning game for young players, and an illustration of how to make factual, scientific information easily 'digestible'!

We have designed a companion game, to demonstrate how food is used in the body, and to promote young people's interest in taking charge of their own health.

'Fit or Fat?'

The objectives of this game are:

(1) To demonstrate that different people use foods in different ways, depending on their bodies' specific needs.
(2) To emphasize that the various food elements are used by the human body in different ways for different needs.
(3) To encourage good general eating and keep-fit habits.

Any number of students can play this game, which takes about 45 minutes. You will need:

- A chair for each player;
- A pair of dice (with a cup to shake them in);
- A packet of balloons;
- A skipping rope;
- A glass of water;
- A stand-on weighing scale;
- A set of written forfeit cards, as detailed below.
  Forfeits:
  - You are too thin; you need more fat in your diet. Miss a turn to blow up a balloon.
  - You ate a take-away hamburger before dinner. Now you have indigestion. Miss a turn and drink a glass of water.
  - You have been ill. Miss a turn and weigh yourself.
  - Weigh yourself. If you are the right weight for your age and height, advance to the next vacant chair.
  - You are too fat. Miss a turn while skipping.
  - You feel the cold too much; you lack energy. Miss a turn and run right round the circle.
  - You lack muscle. Miss a turn and jog round the circle.
  - What is a calorie? Miss a turn if you cannot answer. (The answer is on the back of the card; a calorie is a measure of energy or heat.)
  - What foods contain protein? Miss a turn if you cannot answer. (The answer is on the back of the card: meat, fish, eggs, cheese, grains and nuts.)
  - Why do you need carbohydrate in your diet? Miss a turn if you cannot answer. (The answer is on the back of the card: for energy, body warmth, movement, growth, and cellulose for roughage.)
  - How do you prepare food without using much fat? Miss a turn if you cannot answer. (The answer is on the back of the card: by boiling or steaming, cooking in a microwave or broiling in an oven without fat.)

- Name two diseases associated with overweight. Miss a turn if
  you cannot answer. (The answer is on the back of the card: high
  blood pressure, diabetes, cancer, liver disease, gall bladder
  disease, clots in the blood vessels of the brain.)

'Fit or Fat?' is played on the same principle as 'Snakes and Ladders',
in which players advance over a measured distance according to
throws of the dice. If they land on a snake they lose ground and if
they arrive at the foot of a ladder they move up. To play 'Fit or Fat?'
you set up as large a square of chairs as possible, all round the
walls, one chair for every player, all facing inwards to the room.
If you have a lot of players (and therefore a lot of chairs), you can
line the chairs up in the shape of a 'Z', zig-zagging down the room.
In fact, you can set up any arrangement of chairs you like, bearing in
mind that players are going to have to move up and down the line.

Divide the players into two groups of the same size. One group
should seat themselves on every alternate chair. Each of these seated
players is given one or more forfeit cards to hold (you can invent as
many forfeits as you like). All of the chairs represent squares on a
game board and the seated people are the 'snakes' and 'ladders'.

The game players all start at the same point and take turns throwing the dice. The first player to throw a six begins the game by
throwing again, then walking down the line of chairs, or round the
circle as the case may be, counting chairs to the number shown on
the dice. If this player lands on an empty chair, he or she sits on it.
If they land on a seated player then this 'snake' or 'ladder' reads
aloud his or her forfeit, which the player who landed on this 'square'
has to perform before the next player can throw the dice and take a
turn. If the snake or ladder holds more than one forfeit card, the
game player can choose one at random. The first game player to
complete the line or circle is the winner of that round. In Round 2
the game players change places with the snakes and ladders. You can
play as many rounds as you have time for, or the players have
patience for.

One way of evaluating the learning potential of 'Fit or Fat?' is to
distribute a'questionnaire to all the participants, about a week afterwards, rewording the forfeits as questions and leaving a space at the
end for any comments respondents may care to make about playing
the game. Since you have not done any pretesting, you will not really
know how much new information was acquired by the players from
the game but you will get some idea of the kind of learning, if any,
they have absorbed if you study their replies qualitatively as well as
quantitatively.

For example, you could ask: 'How can you help your body to
build more muscle? Give at least one example'. If the respondent
replies: 'Jogging' it is probably reasonable to assume they learned

that from the game, but you may be able to check on this personally with the individual student. It is very difficult — some would say impossible — to assess the learning components of any exercise in isolation. There are many books available which make the attempt, but when it comes to evaluating games, we think the best is still the one written by Campbell and Stanley in 1963, called *Experimental and Quasi-Experimental Designs for Research.* It is nothing to do with games as such, but it describes clearly a number of research designs that can be adapted by games leaders with relative ease.

We have also invented or adapted some methods of our own. One is to offer young respondents a number of line drawings of faces, all with different expressions. One face is smiling happily, another has question marks coming out of it in all directions, another is frowning and angry-looking, and so on. We ask the students to pick the face that best reflects their own feelings, and then encourage them to tell us why. Another method is to ask the students to write an essay describing their experiences in the game. In Chapter Seven we describe the results when a teacher asked her class to do this after playing one of our games called 'New Year's Eve Hat'.

Because we have been playing learning games internationally for a number of years, we quite often meet up again with educators and business people who remind us they once participated in a particular game with us. These people often use the same words on these occasions. They say: 'I'll never forget...' and then go on to describe what it was they found so memorable about the experience. Sometimes we ask them: 'What do you think you learned from that?' and we usually get a reply that satisfies us. For example, one man, referring to 'Smarties', said: 'I think it taught me a lot about negotiation. I know that ever since playing that game I've looked for people's "hidden agendas" when I'm dealing with them.'

Of course, one cannot legitimately extrapolate from so little data, but it is arguable that feedback like this, over a long period of time, is perhaps the most cogent reason for teachers to continue using games as learning strategies. Teaching can, in some ways, be compared to marketing. It is a relatively easy matter to sell anything once, but when customers keep coming back for more, retailers become aware that they must be doing something right. Perhaps the fact that we are still 'in business' is the best reference we can offer for the effectiveness of games such as those we have already described, and those in the following chapters.

Chapter 4

Money Games

In industrialized societies, money is power; and government, educational and business organizations are microcosms of the societies that sustain them. Therefore, we find that money games are effective devices to use in leadership development programmes to foster learning about the acquisition and uses of power.

All of the games in this chapter are short; none of them will take longer than two hours to play and debrief. This is because we do not want to generate more learning material than we think we can usefully process in one session. You will note when you get to Chapter Six that when we direct longer games we tend to stop the play every 20 minutes or so and discuss what has happened so far before continuing with the action. We believe that this is also an effective procedure for the following games.

All but one of them involve players in actual gains and losses, either of money or — what we have found is the next best inducement after money — sweets or chocolate. Some people might think that playing games for chocolates is a very childish pursuit and quite unsuitable for responsible leadership trainees, but all we can say is that no one ever seems to find it so. Also, as we mentioned in Chapter One, some training groups may contain people who disapprove of anything that seems like gambling for money, in which case colourful, sugar-coated chocolate pieces are a very useful substitute. In the United States these sweets are called M&M's, while in England and Australia they are called Smarties — hence the name of one of the games in this chapter. They have the great advantage that they do not melt or get sticky in the warmth of the classroom, or in people's hands. Both money and chocolate add urgency and importance to quite simple games, and this turns them into potent teaching tools.

There is, however, one game that cannot be played with anything except real money, and that is 'Auction', which is based on a game called 'The Game of Life', in Michael Laver's book, *Playing Politics* (1979).

'Auction'

This game needs from about seven players up to any number, and
£3 for each player. Do not worry about the money — you will get it
all back. All the players are seated at one table (though if there is a
large number of people, several games can be played simultaneously
at different tables). Either you will be the banker or some other
disinterested party will be, who must then be briefed in advance.
You should have prepared a list of rules of the game, one copy for
each player, to read as follows:

(1) Each player receives £1 in coins from the Bank of Life. Any
    currency may be used. If Smarties are used, give each player ten
    of them.
(2) At the start of each round, each player who wants to be in the
    game must put 10 pence (or one Smartie) in a central fund,
    which is placed in the middle of the table.
(3) The Bank will match these resources penny for penny, adding the
    money to the central fund.
(4) Players then bid for this fund. Players can bid any sum in mul-
    tiples of ten pence, but must place it in front of them on the
    table. If they wish to raise a previous bid, they must put the
    additional amount in front of them. No bid may be withdrawn
    once the money is on the table.
(5) The entire central fund is paid out to the player making the
    highest bid.
(6) All bids are then forfeited and returned to the Bank of Life.
(7) Deals and side payments between players are allowed, but *no
    deal is enforceable*.
(8) Bids may be made only by *individuals* and the central fund may
    be won by only *one person*.
(9) At the end of each round, once the pay-out has been made,
    and after a short period of negotiation, if the players want it,
    Round 2 will begin as in Round 1, starting at (2) above.

Let us assume that you are playing with a group of 20 people.
Give them each £1 in small change (to be returned to you at the end
of the game). Each person puts 10 pence in the central fund. This is
not a bid; this sum is their contribution in order to be in the game.
Thus, in this instance there is £2 in the fund, to which you, as
banker, add £2 and then call for bids for this £4 pot. Sooner or later
someone will bid, say, 10 pence by placing it in front of them on the
table, and then the rest will start joining in. At this point, some
agitated discussion usually begins as players seek clarification from
each other about the economic possibilities of the game.

When no one is willing to bid anymore, you give the £4 pot to the highest individual bidder, and scoop up *all* the money on the table (including the successful bid). Keep referring people to the rules if you have any argument (see rule (6) in this case). Start Round 2 as soon as you can, pushing people along a bit if you have to (but allow them time to form coalitions. Some players may want to leave the room for a few moments for private bargaining; allow this).

Again there may be £4 in the pot (or more or less, depending on whether some people who remained as observers during Round 1 now wish to play, or whether some players wish to become observers and conserve their resources). By now at least one, and usually more, of the players have realized that if everyone cooperates, they can break the bank quite quickly. All they have to do, each round, is to allow one person in turn — for as many rounds as there are players — to win the pot on a ten-pence bid.

There are one or two minor problems: for instance, each player only has £1, so if their money runs out before it is their turn to win they will have to trust one of the winners to pay ten pence in order for them to stay in the game. Nevertheless, in theory the above strategy will inevitably bankrupt the bank.

The first time we ever played the game, a couple of players started arguing along these lines, and we became afraid that, as the Bank, we were going to be made fools of. We started thinking frantically about what sort of learning lesson we could draw from this humiliation, but it did not happen and now we can report, dozens of games later, that 'Auction' seldom works that way. Some people can never resist the temptation to try and win more than the others, and so they make deals and then go back on them. Some people are distrustful of others in the first place and refuse to allow them to win by default; and so on. The game starts with a group of isolated individuals. The players must cooperate or all will lose their money, but each must beat the others in order to win.

It is a fascinating game to watch and listen to, especially when there is a really large group, say over 30 players. This is a game that can be videotaped very effectively. Factions form and re-form, leaders rise and fall, trust is established and then broken, sometimes later to be rebuilt, sometimes not. Players argue with each other, and sometimes become angry out of all proportion to the monetary value of the stakes. The exceptions are Japanese players. They are the only people, in our experience, who have broken 'Auction's' bank. This is not inevitable, however, because Japanese like to play power games as much as anybody else, and some groups of Japanese businessmen turn out to be more reckless gamblers even than Australians.

Nevertheless, we remember in particular one Japanese group which realized very quickly how to win the game. One player was delegated (after discussion and consensus agreement) to be the only bidder while the others watched the inevitable result with keen interest. When the bank was broken, the winner scrupulously divided the spoils, the other participants carefully pocketed the money and then looked at us expectantly, waiting to be told what useful lesson they had learned.

One time we played this game with a group of senior trainers, and when it was over we asked them if they thought it had any value for them as a diagnostic training device; but they had all become so involved in the game that it was difficult for them to regain objectivity (another example of the need for *uninvolved observers* of simulations, games, and role-plays as teaching tools). So we replayed the videotape, which led to a very interesting discussion. For example, one of the players — a training manager in real life for a large bank — said that it had been very interesting for her to observe the reckless behaviour of several people who apparently developed 'gambling fever'. They took money out of their own pockets to remain in the game after losing their initial stakes (in fact, this often happens but this observer could not have been expected to know that. She had herself been a very cautious player).

This woman concluded that games might be a valuable diagnostic tool within her own training programmes. For example, playing 'Auction' had already given her the idea of designing a seminar to be called something like, 'Human Factors in Funding Decisions', to be based on company policy. She said this kind of spin-off from games might raise her credit with her boss, who might regard her as being perceptive and innovative concerning company training needs.

There is another, simpler, power game that can easily be played with Smarties or money. It is called 'Making Money' and has an even more open structure than 'Auction'. It elicits widely divergent behaviour from the players, whose differences can usefully be discussed afterwards in terms of personal power.

'Making Money'

The goal of this game is to study power, and any number of people can play. You will need about £1 per person, preferably contributed by group members themselves. However, for various reasons you may wish either to provide the money yourself or to distribute a handful of Smarties to each player (the same number for each). If you are using money, remember to have lots of small change. You will also need a blackboard or flipchart to record the results of each round of the game.

Divide the players into groups of three to seven people. Each player should begin the first round with the same individual stake, say 20 pence broken down into even smaller change, or 20 Smarties. Tell everyone that the person in each group (or maybe two people if the group is large) who has the most money (or chocolates) by the end of a ten-minute round will be the leader for the next round and will be able to set the rules for that round. Any form of trading, borrowing, gambling, stealing, begging, etc, is permitted. At the end of ten minutes, call all the groups to order and post the sum of each person's resources. If there are a great many people, get someone to help you.

Now announce that the richest people in each group are the leaders for the next round and they now have the right to set the rules of play; however, every player's objective will be the same as before, namely, to end the round with more money than anyone else. Ask all the leaders to leave the room to discuss their strategies for the next round. They may choose any tactics to keep their leadership (and wealth) — though we find that when we play 'Making Money' with young people (in youth groups or schools, for example) we sometimes have to ban more violent forms of coercion by leaders and/or resistance by group members.

Give the leaders five minutes or so to consider strategies, then recall them, put them back in their groups, give them a few minutes to explain to their members what the new rules are, and begin Round 2, announcing that the leadership may change at the end of the round, depending on the distribution of resources. Theoretically, the leadership should not change in any group, because the people who emerged as leaders should now formalize the rules so that inevitably they get richer and the rest get poorer. However, this does not always happen, usually because some group members become as smart at playing the game as the leaders, and find ways to circumvent the new rules in their own favour.

Play as many rounds as the players ask for, or have time for, or that you think are sufficient for your teaching aims; and then debrief the game in terms of leadership and persuasive skills. You should be able to point out that the most successful leaders — that is, the ones who become richest — are those people who are best able to achieve one of two situations. Either their followers *actively cooperate* to enrich the leader because in return the followers get some kind of reward themselves, or they defer to the leader out of respect and/ or fear.

In one game that we played, one man eventually became the manager of the whole group, not just his own sub-group, because he opened a 'Two-Up' school. This is a very popular Australian pastime in which people bet on whether a tossed coin will fall heads or tails up — and the person who runs the school always takes a cut of the profits, so this man became very rich but, even more important, his followers were kept very happy in the process.

The other situation in which emergent leaders manage successfully to formalize their positions is through overt use of power, prestige, class or status, so that no one feels assertive enough to oppose them. This can happen, for example, if you are directing a group of employees of widely different status within the same company. The junior trainees are not likely to oppose a bid for leadership if it comes from someone much older, or someone who has been with the company for 20 years (though it can happen, if the juniors are aggressive and ambitious). In an Australian setting, Asian students are less likely than the native white Australians to challenge an emergent leader, and so on.

It is always important to have plenty of time for debriefing. The fun of the game must not detract from the emphasis being placed on leadership skills.

The following is another power game you might like to try, this time concerning the process of group decision-making.

'Money in the Middle'

This game will take any time from less than five minutes to nearly an hour, depending on how many people there are in the group (any number over five can play), and how quickly they reach consensus. It can be played anywhere, so long as the players can sit in one big circle with the 'money in the middle'. It is not a gambling game, so no one should be offended when you ask each participant to contribute 20 pence — though they will not get the money back. If someone does not have twenty pence, *give* him or her the money (make it clear you are not lending it) to put in the pot.

Sit everyone in a circle; this is important. Put the money in the middle, visible to all and accessible to all. Announce that one person, and only one, will get it all, to spend as he or she likes, though not to return to the individuals who donated it. Then do not say anything else. After a silence, someone will probably ask who the lucky person will be. Answer that this is for the group to decide, but *there must be consensus*. Again, do not say anything more.

Groups solve this problem in different ways. Sometimes an emergent leader or leaders devise some sort of game and give the money to the winner. This is the simplest, quickest, and most equitable solution, and one which is the most fun. We are always surprised that groups do not think of it more often. If people start talking about who deserves it most, for instance, they inevitably get bogged down and the discussion can last a long time. Sometimes a person will just take the money and defy anyone to get it back.

We remember a group of middle managers actually engaging in a

physical fight because one of them put the money in his pocket   an
example of a bid for power that was too overt to work *with that
particular group*. The man was a poor psychologist. His bluff might
have worked with a group of people who were not his peers, or who
were not as assertive as he. If a power play like this is successful, do
not let it worry you. Just announce the end of Round 1 and start all
over again. You will find the tension noticeably higher in Round 2 as
the players start looking for ways to take revenge on the deviant.

When the decision has finally been made, ask the participants who
or what the real decision-maker was. What happened? Help them
retrace the argument and discuss their feelings. How were priorities
established? Did any one person set them, or a sub-group of people,
openly or tacitly? There are other questions that can usefully be
asked, concerning individual problem-solving styles, for example,
such as enquiring who pressed for solutions and closure, and who
widened the scope of the debate. Who spoke most? Who listened
most? And what were people's feelings as the game was played?
Allow enough time for people to think about these questions, bearing
in mind that some people take longer than others to 'get going'.

'The Five-Pound Note'

Another good negotiation game is one that we have adapted from a
game by Martin Belbin. The game leader auctions £5, and so we call
the game 'The Five-Pound Note'. The bids have to be in 10-pence
offers and you have to make it clear that all bids are forfeit to you as
auctioneer. Belbin suggests that players may be more keen to make
their opponents lose than they are to win themselves, but in our
experience the players are torn between wanting to win and wanting
to beat, not each other, but us.

'The Five-Pound Note' is an entrepreneurial game because players
recognize that it makes the best sense not to play; this, however,
applies to the others as well, so maybe they should play after all.
Belbin relates the outcomes of the game to real-world negotiations
like the arms race, wars in different parts of the world, and union-
management disputes. He suggests that these are the issues that the
game leader should raise with the group. However, we are more
interested in making the following points:

(1) It is hard to let go of a situation in which you have already
    invested time and trouble, and in this case money. This feeling
    may tempt you to 'hang in there' longer than you can afford. On
    the other hand, if you are willing to invest your resources only
    up to a certain level, which you have decided in advance, you
    can relax, enjoy the activity and learn a lot about negotiation.

(2) If you are afraid you are getting in too deep, but feel it is too late to withdraw, your opponents will sense this and increase their bids. On the other hand, if you can bring yourself to withdraw when the going gets too hot for you, you may lose some money, because your bids will have been forfeited to the auctioneer, but you will have learned something about the other players, and yourself. In addition, you will know how to recognize in the future the characteristics of escalation games, so you can avoid them if you want to.

'Quote Me a Price'

We have also devised a role-play to demonstrate negotiation skills, and it always seems to work effectively. We call it 'Quote Me a Price'. We set the scene, putting a player in a role as a salesperson in a second-hand, bric-a-brac shop where bargaining between buyer and seller is common practice. We use furnishings from around the room, and borrow bits and pieces from players to provide the stock; and add a very pretty glass paperweight that we bring for these occasions. Then we ask (or tell) somebody to be a buyer who has seen this paperweight in the shop window, has taken a real fancy to it and enters the shop determined to purchase it at a reasonable cost. Buyer and seller have to decide privately what they think is 'reasonable'.

We video this role-play and then debrief it via the playback, stopping the tape when we see something we particularly want to draw to the attention of the viewers. For example, one buyer began by saying: 'I'll give you £1 for that paperweight', which alerted the seller to his 'bottom line'; so she made an extreme counter-offer, £5, and rode out the buyer's derision (in fact, she handled stress very well throughout). When the purchaser dug his heels in, so did she, and appeared willing to break off the negotiations if all he would offer was £1. He modified his stand and raised the offer to £1.50. At this point, she called on the services of another player in the shop and announced him as a world authority on paperweights, who would attest to the value of this one. The buyer accepted the word of the disinterested expert but enlarged the scope of the debate by saying that he was a regular customer and it was in her interests to keep him satisfied. At this point, she said that she would have to talk to her manager, and handed over the negotiations to another player.

The manager expressed every desire to satisfy this valued client and added all sorts of extra information about the paperweight's previous owner, now unfortunately deceased but formerly a wealthy and discerning collector. He waxed eloquent about the quality of its glass and the beauty of its design until the customer raised his offer to £2. After that there was a pattern of negotiation with the manager suggesting £5.50 and the buyer £3, until eventually they agreed on the seller's original price of £5. It was interesting to see how the intervals of time between offers and counter-offers became less and less the nearer they got to agreement. Moreover, the manager helped the buyer to save face over having to pay the original price; he refrained from the slightest suggestion of gloating and congratulated his customer on having made an excellent purchase.

These players were all experienced negotiators in real life and it was highly enlightening to see how well they handled this role-play. On another occasion, when the players were not so skilful, they were less able to signal their commitments and the transaction was in danger of foundering. We suggested that they might enlarge the scope of the discussion by adding a contingency arrangement, such as the possibility of the customer returning the paperweight if he or she was not entirely happy with it. This spurred the buyer on to offer to sell the paperweight at the lower figure if the customer would agree to purchase something else in the shop as well — which is what happened.

In summary, you can use this game to illustrate the basics of negotiation, which are:

(1) Beware of opening first with a concrete offer; it may 'anchor' your adversary's perceptions.
(2) Gauge your reactions to an extreme suggestion. Either break off negotiations until the other side modifies its stand, or make a counter-offer and expect to end up somewhere between the two. Be aware of your own aspiration level, and protect your integrity.
(3) Keep reassessing your perceptions, and learn to recognize patterns of concessions. Your concessions should be paced and linked to those of your adversary. Note that the intervals between offers should become shorter as limits are signalled. Learn to handle stress.
(4) Signal your commitments. Make it clear when you will go no further (whether, in fact, this is true or not). Learn to communicate your intentions effectively with non-verbal behaviour as well as words.
(5) Introduce a disinterested or expert third party as a mediator.
(6) Enlarge the scope of the negotiation, for instance, by including contingency arrangements.
(7) If you want to avoid being pushed into a commitment, or if you want to change your mind, you can do several things. For example, you can:
- get yourself replaced by another negotiator;
- state that you have received new instructions and/or information;
- include new issues in the debate.

(8) Help your adversaries to save face. For example:
- agree that the circumstances have changed, even if they have not, which makes your adversaries' change of mind perfectly reasonable;
- accept that they were pushed for time and were not able to prepare properly to negotiate with you.

(9) Do not gloat.

You can set up a variation of 'Quote Me a Price' by asking two players to divide £2 between them, and by penalizing one of them 5 pence per minute of negotiation and the other 10 pence per minute. This is a neat little exercise for players to practice bluff as well as 'thinking on their feet'. The player who stands to lose more from delay is theoretically in a weaker bargaining position. This person often does end up with virtually nothing out of the £2. However, if players in this position can think fast enough to say something like: 'The longer we stand here talking the more money we both lose. How about if you take 10 per cent extra for your cut?', they have a good chance of getting away with a payout of 80 pence, which under the circumstances could have been a lot higher.

We originally designed our next game, 'Smarties', for occupational health students, to give them some experience of leadership in problems related to occupational safety hazards, when remedies are likely to be in opposition to management policy, ie when remedies are likely to interfere with productivity. We have since adapted it to be relevant to any organizational experience where workers' welfare and management aims are in opposition, in order to help management and leadership trainees find ways to reconcile their opposing aims. As we mentioned above, it may seem a childish exercise to ask grown men and women to eat as many Smarties as they can — so maybe you will not want to play this game until you are on terms of trust and esteem with your group — but we can practically guarantee that nobody will find it undignified.

'Smarties'

Any number of people can play this power game, but the absolute minimum is eight and you will need lots of space in the room. Stack the chairs in the hall if necessary. The materials are as follows:

(1) Literally thousands of 'Smarties' (M&M's), many of which are going to be eaten. Fortunately they are not expensive.
(2) A large container of water or a soft drink (unless you want to supply alcoholic refreshment, in which case the game will take on an added dimension) and enough plastic cups for everyone. You

will also need plenty of plastic cups on the main playing table for people to use as containers for their Smarties.

(3) About £10 changed into 1-pence pieces (you may need more, but you will get it all back. We have commented before on the psychological advantages of using real money in these learning games).

Put any six players in roles as: two managers, two workers, and a character who symbolizes the social pressures of a consumer society. There is also a union representative, conservationist, environmentalist, or some such character who is concerned to protect workers and the general public from the forces of production. If you have lots of people, create more social pressures and more workers before you add an extra manager. All other participants are consumers.

The six main characters sit and stand round the playing table on which there is literally a mountain of Smarties. When people remain standing to play a game, they are more likely to use body language, such as gestures or touching each other, perhaps to restrain someone physically, in this game, from eating the Smarties.

The two managers are given all the money (they operate in partnership) and also a bag of Smarties in case the mountain becomes eroded and needs rebuilding. The consumers either sit in a larger circle around the table and its occupants, or they may prefer to wander around, watching and listening to the action. The refreshment stand is located somewhere off to the side, and we usually act as the waiters because we like to have a small piece of the action, but you may prefer to delegate this task to one of the observers. The aims and objectives of the characters are as follows:

(1) The managers want the workers to prepare Smarties for workers and consumers to eat (the managers do not eat Smarties themselves, because their job is to produce, not consume these lowly articles). They have to decide what wages to pay, but a good estimate is 10 pence for every 100 Smarties consumed.

(2) The workers have to collect as many Smarties as they think will be consumed, take the container to one of the managers for checking, and then either eat the smarties themselves or offer them to the consumers. Before managers pay out the appropriate sum for the number consumed, they should keep an eye on the action to make sure no Smarties have been thrown away or otherwise illegally disposed of — they have to be *eaten*. You may prefer to keep track of this yourself, or to ask observers to see that the people who take the Smarties actually put them in their mouths and swallow them. The managers' most urgent priority is *maximum consumption*. As a bonus for good work, they can invite workers and/or consumers to be their guests at

the refreshment buffet (only the managers can help themselves to drinks; others must be invited).

(3) The union representative (or conservationist or whoever) has read a report that the Smarties are carcinogenic, and does not want anyone to eat any more until extensive health tests have been carried out. Meanwhile, the production lines should be shut down. The most urgent priority is *nil consumption*.

(4) The character who symbolizes the consumer society wants to put as much pressure as possible on workers and consumers to eat more and more Smarties; this person goes around suggesting ways they can do so.

(5) The workers know that if their leaders become dissatisfied with their performance and dismiss them, there are plenty of consumers who are ready to take their place on the production line.

Anyone can talk to anyone else; any syndicates, pressure groups, etc, can be formed; anyone can do virtually anything within the above general context. You may want to write out all the main roles individually, adding any extra comments or colourful touches of your own, in which case presumably no one will start off knowing the motives of the other characters; or you can describe the scenario aloud to everyone in your own words; with as much eloquence as you can muster.

We think it is more effective to describe everything verbally to everyone, but the really important thing is to motivate the participants to play their roles with enthusiasm. Thus, you should either write something to this effect into the roles or give the group a pep-talk before you start the game. In any case, the presence of the Smarties will add to your persuasions, because they always seem to exercise a powerful motivating force on the players.

However you set it up, the result will probably be noisy, which is fine. You want the managers to encourage the workers to get more and more Smarties eaten — with offers of refreshments, higher wages, bonuses and incentives for increased consumption. They may set one worker in competition against another, and so on. On the other hand, the union representative or conservationist utters grim warnings; while all the time the consumer society tempts the workers to eat more and earn more. Everyone usually ends up shouting and frequently the observers join in.

Let the game run its course. There are many possible outcomes because the structure of the game is open. Maybe all the Smarties will be eaten, or they may be forgotten in the heat of debate. The workers and consumers may listen to the union representative, who may, as a result, succeed in getting the Smarties banned (and may even force the managers to suggest another form of labour); and so on.

On one occasion when we played the game with a group of
physical education teachers, the workers, under pressure from the
consumers as well as the union representative, abandoned the Smarties and used sheets from their notepads to make paper hats to 'sell'
for a 'crippled children's association'. They did so with the full
cooperation of the management, who agreed to pay the same wages
as before, and everyone ended up wearing a paper hat. Sometimes
the people are swayed by the social pressures of the consumer
society and eat the Smarties as fast as they can. The workers refuse
to listen to any health warnings because they argue that otherwise
they will lose their jobs and they cannot afford to be out of work.
Sometimes a pressure group of consumers will side with the conservationist and get the workers 'laid off'; then they negotiate with
the managers to make some nominal safety changes and take over the
jobs themselves, and so on.

The discussion afterwards is likely to be animated. We vividly
remember one senior nurse on an occupational health course who
played the role of a health officer (equivalent to the role of union
representative). She completely failed in her efforts (which became
quite frantic as the game progressed) to stop people eating the
Smarties. This was largely because the woman who played the
consumer society was so persuasive. She interpreted her role by
presenting what were, in effect, a series of commercials about the
lovely things the workers could buy with their wages, and how good
chocolate was nutritionally for the consumers.

The nurse said afterwards that the game had given her such a sense
of helplessness and frustration that she felt ready to burst into tears
as the table became more and more empty of Smarties. She said she
now felt much more able to identify with the efforts of conservationists and other members of the real-life community who work against
all the pressures of a consumer society to protect the quality of
people's lives.

This kind of reaction, and the various responses of all the players
and observers, can be related to the theme of power. In other words,
how did the characters structure the action? Who controlled whom?
Why? How did the various characters perceive their tasks? How did
the consumers perceive the behaviour of the characters? What we
hope for, when we direct this game, is that participants will begin to
consider the sociopolitical contexts in which organizational power
operates, and to become more aware that the extent to which
individuals can control this context governs the degree of power they
can achieve.

We also find 'Smarties' to be a game that can usefully begin a
session on stress management in organizational settings, because we
argue that personal stress is directly related to three interacting

factors: the degree of importance of the situation to the stresses; the degree of personal authority to control it; and the degree of access to company corridors of power, ie where the real decision-making takes place. Thus in 'Smarties', union representatives, for example, will be in a relatively stress-free situation if they do not really care whether the workers get cancer (especially as they themselves are under no compulsion to eat any Smarties) and/or, if they can organize a body of supporters to put pressure on the managers. On the other hand, workers can find themselves genuinely under stress in the game if they listen to the dire warnings about cancer, yet feel powerless to avoid the pressures of the managers and the consumer society.

Another money game we like very much is 'The Road Game' (Lineham and Long, 1970), which is another of the few games described in this book that we did not invent ourselves; we merely adapted it to our teaching needs. As well as being about power, it is about economic imperatives, pressures of public opinion, and priorities concerning quality of life. It is a good game for increasing people's awareness that there are *choices* involved, on several levels, in any development programme for a company, organization, neighbourhood, city or nation.

'The Road Game'

You will need a lot of players for this — within limits, the more the merrier. It works very well with a group of about 20 to 35 people, though it can be played with an absolute minimum of eight — but try to get hold of at least 12. It is a good game to play at a conference, because you have access to numbers of people, and they will very likely enjoy discussing it on and off for days. It takes about two hours to play and requires the following materials:

(1) Four sheets of thin drawing cardboard (20 x 24 cm or any size convenient for you), the sort you buy from an art supply shop or from your local stationer. Each sheet should be a different colour.
(2) Sticky or masking tape to join the four sheets of cardboard together to make one huge square. This is the playing board.
(3) Four fat felt-tipped pens, preferably in the colours of the four cardboard sheets, but it does not really matter so long as they are each a different colour.

'The Road Game' is best played with the big board on a carpeted floor with lots of space all around so people can walk, kneel, or crawl as they feel like it. However, if there is no carpet on the floor, put the board on a table approximately the same size as the board, and let people stand around it. Explain that the four coloured squares on the board are four countries and the players are all citizens of one country or another. Let them divide themselves up any way they like; it does not really matter if the populations are not evenly distributed.

Every citizen of every country has to pay a capital sum into the World Bank — you can ask for any sum that seems suitable, from about 30 pence upwards. If you are playing with a group which does not have any money (for example, we have played this game with young people on a retraining programme in a reform school), you will have to put 30 pence per player in the bank yourself. Announce that each country has a leader and a state engineer; everyone else is an ordinary person. Countries can decide which sort of leadership to have and how they are going to decide on their leader and their engineer. Give them five minutes to do this. Then announce that the object of the game is to build roads, and give a felt-tipped pen to each state engineer, emphasizing that only engineers can put pen to board.

The rules are simple. Any completed road earns 20 pence from the World Bank to be paid to the country that built it. To be classed as 'completed', a road must begin somewhere in the country of owner-ship and end at the edge of the playing board *in someone else's country* (internal roads do not count). Before crossing any frontier, the road builders must first obtain the permission of the leader of the country into which they wish to extend their road. If road builders want to cross a road belonging to another country, *even if that road is on their own land*, the same negotiation process must take place.

The number of completed roads will be tallied at the end of the game and the monies paid out. However, there will be an oppor-tunity for any country to protest that another country's roads were built illegally, and if the protest is upheld at the World Court, the relevant road is erased and that country does not get the money.

Only state engineers can draw roads, and only leaders can negoti-ate between countries. Emphasize the game's few rules, and the definition of a completed road, as strongly as you can. You can write the rules down in advance if you like, and give everyone a copy. Then let everyone get on with it; do not interfere at all, even if the rules are being broken right, left and centre. The game will become a microcosm of power politics and is enthralling to watch and listen to. If numbers are large, many of the players will become observers of the action, while their leaders are negotiating on their behalf; nevertheless, the game is worth videotaping for replay later.

Some countries are indifferent to anything except development, while others seek to protect their environment; and each country will develop power ploys that are worth examining in some detail afterwards. Probably our most effective way to offer suggestions for debriefing 'The Road Game' is to describe the results of a game we played some years ago for an environment protection organization (Stone, 1981).

The four countries, each with about seven citizens, plus their leader and engineer, called themselves respectively Salami, Serenia, Beli Cose, and Kom Erse. The people of Salami decided they were going all out to get rich quick. They would forget about social conscience, civic planning, and preservation of the environment. They did not bother to build any roads at all. Anyone could come on to their land and build roads wherever they pleased — for a price of 8 pence a road, payable in advance.

Serenia decided that it had plenty of natural resources and withdrew from the outside world — no roads in, no roads out. Its people spent the entire game happily breathing down the state engineer's neck while she crawled around drawing houses and trees to their instructions, and churches and hospitals, animals, and a countryside with lots of windmills and waterfalls and solar catchment areas. The citizens of Beli Cose took a pragmatic stand: this is a game, they said. The object of the game is to draw as many roads as possible. 'Right,' they said, 'that's what we'll do'.

Their leader soon found out that Serenia was not interested in letting anyone cross her borders, and that Kom Erse would consider roads only on a one-for-one basis, which left Salami. Both Beli Cose and Kom Erse fell on Salami with cries of joy when they realized she would agree to anything. Kom Erse tried to haggle over the price, however, which was a tactical error, because the leader of Beli Cose took 10 pence out of her own purse and gave it to the leader of Salami, saying grandly: 'Keep the change!'. Then she rapidly moved her state engineer in, to draw a blue road in such a way that Kom Erse would have to cross it (and therefore would need Beli Cose's permission) to get to Salami's perimeter. Kom Erse was furious and its citizens loudly abused their leader for being outsmarted. However, he was not far behind. He promptly paid for a road, so close to Beli Cose's borders that the balance of power was restored because Beli Cose would have to cross it to get virtually anywhere. After that the two countries worked out some kind of bargaining system in an atmosphere of 'cold war' negotiation.

In addition to getting him to draw roads, Kom Erse's citizens also kept their engineer busy siting cities and industrial centres and airports. But Beli Cose's leader loved the diplomatic process *per se* and spent all her time in close consultation with other heads of state. Her people saw very little of her so, though her engineer tried to create the site for a capital city, it never really got off the ground. Other considerations always came first with the leader, like trying to fit in another road without crossing an existing one. She kept making unilateral decisions and telling the people about them afterwards, when it was too late to protest.

At the end of about an hour we called a halt, even though the game had got to a stage where Beli Cose's leader was looking greedily at Serenia's empty spaces; but the debriefing of 'The Road Game' is every bit as important as playing it, and we did not want to cut that time short by continuing to play. Salami was the official winner, with capital reserves of £1.28, and no one could accuse her of behaving illegally because she had not built any roads. However, ecologically it was a mess, with lots of foreign-built roads all over the place. Salami's citizens did not care. They announced that they were all in voluntary and luxurious exile in the Bahamas.

Beli Cose came second, with £1.08 and a half-built capital city. They would have earned more, but Kom Erse protested that one of their roads had been drawn without consent, and Serenia and Salami upheld the protest. Kom Erse was third with 84 pence, but insisted it had won overall because it was the only country with an international road transport system, money *and* an environment. Serenia had no money at all, but was quite unrepentant. Its people had done their own thing and were feeling very pleased with themselves — though they looked rather thoughtful when the leader of Beli Cose agreed with us that she would have followed the call of *lebensraum* and invaded Serenia if time had permitted.

The three 'losers' (but what does 'losing' mean in the context of the game?) were unanimous in condemning Salami's foreign and domestic policies, in spite of (or because of?) the fact that Salami had 'won'.

Debriefing 'The Road Game' should be organized so that each country takes its turn to comment on the game, if they wish, to complain about the behaviour of another country, or countries, one at a time. The two countries who are not immediately involved in the dispute are the judges, who must decide whether the relevant country gets paid for its roads. As game directors, we structure the discussion, but do not take part in it except to ask questions. We guarantee that the debate will offer a great many insights to organizational (ie political) behaviour, though sometimes we have to be the ones to draw these observations to the attention of the group.

For instance, on another occasion when we played this game, one very senior lecturer in a university teaching seminar expressed derision over it — he said crawling all over the floor was a game for children, that the activity was totally disorganized, and that no one could possibly learn anything from it. We asked him to be patient and listen to the discussion. By the end of half an hour he had quietened down considerably and when the seminar was over he stayed behind to ask if we had any more political games.

'The Road Game', like all the other money games in this chapter, is also useful if you want to make a number of theoretical points, derived from leadership literature, because the examples will be there, ready for you to refer back to. For instance, two of our favourite theorists are Fiedler and Chemers (1974), and the following are some of their arguments that we find players unwittingly support by their behaviour when they play money games:

- In the first place, they assume a relationship between people in which influence and power are unevenly distributed on a legitimate basis, that is, by the consent of group members, by contract or by law; and they say that players who emerge as group leaders, in games like 'Making Money' and 'Money in the Middle', do so first through (tacit) group consent; then (as in 'Money in the Middle' and 'Smarties') they maintain their leadership status (if they do) through the rules they themselves impose.
- They suggest that a leader's followers must implicitly or explicitly consent to their part in the arrangement by relinquishing to the leader their right to make independent decisions. We constantly see this happening in money games, though occasionally there is open rebellion and the leader is overthrown. This nearly happened, for example, to the leader of Kom Erse in the playing of 'The Road Game' described above. The reason it did not is that he took rapid and visibly effective action to validate and maintain his formal leadership status, ie he restored the balance of power between his country and its rival, which satisfied his citizens that he was competent as a leader.
- If rebellion does not happen, they argue, it is because there is an *exchange* between leaders and followers. In 'Making Money', for example, the leaders get the tangible rewards of money or chocolates, plus intangibles such as a sense of success — what psychologists call a 'psychic income'. This means that leaders become emotionally involved in leadership, while their followers appear to gain a sense of security — frequently described by them as a feeling that a game is 'more fun' when it is organized by an efficient leader.

These ideas, all highly relevant to leadership training programmes, make for vigorous discussions between players after money games. It may also be worth drawing their attention to the phenomenon that some real-life managers, even though they have leadership *status*, are not effective managers. The difference can be demonstrated in games, because the groups with more effective leaders will be more productive in terms of the game's objectives. Their group members are also more likely to feel satisfied at the end of the game. This does not necessarily mean that they will feel happier or more comfortable, but that they will leave the session with a feeling of real accomplishment — that they have learned something new or achieved some goal. This result occurs only when group leaders are concerned with more than their own status.

Also in money games it seems easy to see the distinction between the concepts of *emergent* and *formal* leaders. For instance, if there are any leaders among the players of 'Making Money', they become so by emerging out of the group, with its tacit consent, and only later do they move to formalize their position by imposing rules, sometimes successfully, sometimes not. On the other hand, the managers in 'Smarties' and the national leaders in 'The Road Game' are licensed, so to speak, to lead; and whether they maintain their leadership depends on how successfully they can prevent their followers from questioning the assumption of their formal status.

Whether they are emergent or formal, leaders demonstrate certain behaviour which can be observed and identified in magnified and simplified forms through playing games. For example, money games can demonstrate that leaders *emerge* because:

(1) They find that leadership gives them a personal reward, not necessarily financial. This was clearly demonstrated by the leader of Beli Cose in 'The Road Game'. She was more interested in the experience of power than in any other aspect of the game.
(2) They are motivated by a feeling that they can succeed.
(3) They receive acceptance from and support by the group.

Furthermore, all leaders, whether emergent or formal, maintain leadership by:

(1) Group acceptance;
(2) Group satisfaction, which may or may not include tangible profit, though it does so in these money games.
(3) Leaders' ability to satisfy the needs both of their group members and of their superiors.

It is worth noting that this means that in games a group leader must take cognizance of the needs of the game director, who always retains the final power arbitrarily to deprive any player of leadership status. This is another reason why we do not like the word 'facilitator' to describe a game leader's director's behaviour. Players are always aware, at some level, that the game director is the final authority. However, game directors have superiors too. If they can not satisfy their clients, they do not get to play games any more.

We also like to point out, when we debrief power games, that emergent leaders are not *necessarily* the people who are most visible (eg, who sit at the head of the table) — though this does give them an initial advantage, which they may or may not make use of. Also there are other physical, psychological and even geographical circumstances that are favourable to leadership, such as being bigger, quicker off the mark, and louder than other people; also factors such as being closer to the game director in order to get money changed more quickly (in 'Making Money', for example) may contribute to successful leadership. But these advantages will count for little if emergent leaders do not suit their leadership style to the temperament of the group. Authoritarian leaders are likely to be rejected by democratically-minded groups unless they also have persuasive skills.

Leadership style theory focuses on what leaders do, not what they are; it focuses in particular on three categories of behaviour:

(1) Group goal facilitation (problem-solving);
(2) Individual prominence (power);
(3) Group sociability (people).

These three kinds of behaviour can be clearly identified by watching the way people play games. For example, leaders will be more or less heedful of the game's objectives, of their own individual prominence, and of the feelings of the rest of the players, depending on whether they are more concerned to achieve a *task* or form a *group relationship*.

If there is a considerable amount of group consensus about the game's objectives, then an emergent and task-oriented leader will have a relatively easy time because the group will perceive clearly that it is being led towards the accomplishment of a common task. Under these circumstances it is not difficult for a would-be leader to achieve and retain individual prominence; the group will see the leader's goals as its own and there will be a good balance between task and group relationships.

However, in the above money games the task is either relatively unstructured or ambiguous. Therefore, if emergent leaders want to become rich and/or powerful when they play these games, they cannot afford to appear too task-oriented. They have to be on such good terms with the group that they can convince all the other players that it is *in their interests* that their leader makes more money than they do. Otherwise the players will reject the leader. This was illustrated very well by the man who started the 'Two-Up' school in 'Making Money'. The players had so much fun that they did not begrudge him his profit.

On the other hand, if leaders become too concerned about the feelings of their followers, they may achieve a very good relationship with the group but fail to complete the given task. The managers in 'Smarties', for example, will not achieve the high productivity that was the stated objective unless they find some compromise between the safety of their workers and their own management aims — maybe by redefining the nature of the task, as did the group of teachers we referred to above, who made hats to sell instead of eating Smarties.

Thus we agree with Fiedler that there are three essential factors in leadership: the degree of *acceptance* of the group, the *structure* of the task, and the individual *power* of the leader. These are three areas to which we direct the group's attention when we are all analysing, wise in hindsight, what happens when we play power games together.

In the following chapter we offer some suggestions for role-plays that focus on personal communication skills that leaders need if they are to achieve three basic management goals:

(1) Leaders need to develop the power of their personalities in order to be accepted by the group. They must inspire their followers to 'go along with them', not necessarily because they like them (though that helps), but because the followers feel the situation, whatever it is, is safe in their hands.

(2) Leaders need to organize their teams and tasks so that they work with the strengths of their group members and buttress areas where the group is not so strong, thus ensuring a well-motivated team who sees the advantages of working with their leader.

(3) Leaders need to gain as much power as they can through their communication skills with the world in general. They have to make and keep important connections, gain access to important information, and enlarge their abilities to reward and punish their followers.

Therefore, we have called the next chapter 'People Games and Role-Plays'.

Chapter 5

People Games and Role-plays

The first of our 'people games' in this chapter — one that we have played many times with groups of educators, business people, and graduate students — confirms something that we have long felt to be true and that we have tried to share with you in the previous pages: the simplest games often produce the best results.

'Teachers and Learners' is one of those activities of which people say, 'Oh, well, anybody could have thought of that!' Yet it provides clear examples of ways in which effective leaders use personality to support knowledge and experience in powerful combinations that motivate their followers.

'Teachers and Learners'

This game can be played with any number of people and takes from 15 minutes to a couple of hours, depending on how many people you have in the group. Essentially, 'Teachers and Learners' consists of one person, or a team of two or three people, taking it in turns to teach something to the rest of the group. We usually play it with about 12 to 25 people and ask them to form teams of two or three people each, depending on numbers, because the exercise can be rather threatening for individuals on their own unless they have a lot of confidence and/or know each other really well. We give all the teams five to ten minutes for their respective members to get into a huddle and decide what they want to teach. After that everyone gathers together again and the first team (the order of precedence is immaterial) begins a three to five minute instruction to the rest of the group. It may be in the form of a lecture, a demonstration, or an enactment of some kind, depending on what the teachers choose to do.

When all the teams have finished, we conduct an informal, oral 'examination'. Each teacher-team, in the order in which they gave their lesson, returns again to the front of the class and their former 'students' are asked to repeat at least the essence of the 'lesson', add any general comments that occur to them, and give the teachers a round of applause.

We have learned a lot from 'Teachers and Learners': how to choose wine, the quickest way on foot from the university to the bus station, what to do if someone faints in the street, and many other useful things. We have also been the victim of some clever jokes — such as when we were informed most seriously of a secret code that dairy farmers put on milk cartons to identify the herd of cows the milk came from.

If you want to play this game, do not forget to time each team of teachers carefully. You may have to interrupt them sometimes, though often they are so interesting that this is really frustrating. We are usually impressed by the teachers' ability to choose appropriate material and manage it within the tight time constraint. But if you find that some participants have trouble with timing their lessons, remember to include the subject of time-management in your debriefing.

Keep the pace brisk during the 'examination' period. Briefly recapitulate the names of the teachers, then ask the group what they remember about the subject of each lesson. (You may want to take notes for your own reference as the game goes along.) It usually becomes quite obvious which were the most easily remembered and popular subjects and/or teachers.

If you are working with real-life teachers you can initiate a general discussion (without getting too personal) about why some teaching behaviours appear to be more effective than others. Start your participants thinking about the concept of 'teacher as leader'. You may find that some teachers already agree with this concept, some greet it as a new but welcome idea, and some dispute it on ideological grounds. If you do get the third type of reaction, offer instead the suggestion that teachers are managers — which may also come as a new idea to some, but which in general seems more acceptable to those of the 'teachers are facilitators' school of thought.

Whoever your participants are, give them lots of examples from your observation of the various teams' performances to support your argument that there are three critical factors which make for more or less effective management/leadership behaviour. Here are some examples of our own, to give you the general idea:

- *Personal presentation:* We remember one 'teacher' (in real life an analytical chemist) whose sheer charm and persuasiveness resulted in us all sampling a 'cocktail' before he told us how he had made it.
- *Quality of information:* This relates to the leaders' ability to impress people with the quality and amount of their knowledge and experience in a particular area. In 'Teachers and Learners' you will find that there is always at least one 'teacher' who so

obviously knows what he or she is talking about that everbody listens attentively, no matter what the subject.

- *Ability to motivate people to listen and learn:* We remember a 'teacher' who taught us all how to make a very complicated paper aeroplane. In real life, she was employed by a large bank as an instructor in the use of computers but she had been trained originally as a primary school teacher. The quality of her instruction and her ability to judge when an individual needed special attention were superb. She made the exercise not only instructive (everybody could make the aeroplane after five minutes' practice) but thoroughly entertaining.

We can also recommend another game — a very short role-play — that illustrates the powerful effects of people-skills (or 'interpersonal communication skills' if you want to make the subject sound more important). This game dramatically illustrates the following:

- Human behaviour is a constant phenomenon whether the owners are conscious of it or not.
- People cannot *not* behave.
- People signal messages to each other all the time, even when they think they are doing nothing in particular.
- If people want to be leaders — to influence others — they need to become more aware that their slightest behaviour makes an impression of some kind on those who observe it.

'Behave Yourself'

This role-play is for people to play with each other in pairs and then report back to the group on the experience. You will have prepared in advance several sets of instructions. Then you give one role to each member of each pair of players, asking each one to read the instructions privately and then play his or her role accordingly. Here are some examples, but you can make up your own if you prefer to do so (eg, if you have some specific teaching purpose for the game).

Set One

ROLE-PLAYER A:
Start talking to your partner about something that interests you and that you feel confident you can talk about for some time. After three to four minutes, or when you feel you have had enough, exchange roles/papers and start again.

ROLE-PLAYER B:
Say nothing while waiting for your partner to start talking, but look

encouraging. When your partner begins to talk, respond in an interested manner. Look at your partner, smile, nod, ask questions, etc, without trying to take over the conversation. After three to four minutes, or when you feel you have had enough, exchange roles/papers and start again.

Set Two

ROLE-PLAYER A: (as for Set One)

ROLE-PLAYER B:
When your partner starts talking to you, look at her or him expressionlessly, as if challenging your partner to interest you. Continue to stare without saying anything. After three to four minutes or when you feel you have had enough, exchange roles/papers with your partner and start again.

Set Three

ROLE-PLAYER A: (as before)

ROLE-PLAYER B:
When your partner starts talking, listen for moment or two, then start fidgeting, crossing and re-crossing your legs, looking at your wristwatch, turning round to see who else is in the room, etc. If your partner stops talking, say, 'Yes, yes, go on!' but continue to appear inattentive. After three to four minutes, or when you feel you have had enough, exchange roles/papers and start again.

Set Four

ROLE-PLAYER A: (as before)

ROLE-PLAYER B:
Wait until your partner starts talking and then, without actually saying anything, indicate by your movements and expression that you disagree with what your partner is saying. If your partner stops, say something like 'Well, all right, go on!' but continue to appear to disagree. After three to four minutes, or when you feel you have had enough, exchange roles/papers and start again.

Set Five

ROLE-PLAYER A:
Talk to your partner about anything that interests you, but do not look directly at your partner at any time. You can look anywhere else you like — round the room, for example — or keep your eyes down.

After three to four minutes, or when you feel you have had enough, exchange roles/papers and start again.

ROLE-PLAYER B:
When your partner starts talking to you, respond as encouragingly as you can. Try to get a conversation going about your partner's topic. Ask questions, seek clarification, etc. After three to four minutes, or when you feel you have had enough, exchange roles/papers with your partner and start again.

The above should be enough to give you the general purpose of this exercise, which is one of the very few, if not the only one, in this book not allowing for observer roles as such. This is because it is important that everybody in the group experiences some kind of personal communication interaction. The role-plays are followed by a general discussion in which players share the contents of their instruction papers and describe what happened during their respective dialogues.

You may find that some people are revealed as such self-absorbed talkers that their listeners virtually have to get up and walk away before the speakers become aware of their boredom and inattention. On the other hand, some people find it really difficult to give these signals because in real life their habit is to continue to present an appearance of interest even if they are bored out of their minds. Not surprisingly, these passive listeners are often women because more women than men are socialized early to be good listeners. However, women can also be very determined talkers.

'Behave Yourself' is an effective role-play because the talkers usually experience — and later describe — strong negative or positive feelings as a result of the way their listeners respond to them. And the listeners will describe how more or less easy it was to obey the instructions on their paper, depending on the behaviour of the talkers.

A good game to follow 'Behave Yourself' is this next one, which we call 'The Photocopy Machine'. We have already referred to it indirectly in the introduction, when we talked about different problem-solving styles and how these can be illustrated by the ways people solve the not unusual problem of the office photocopy machine breaking down. This game is designed to examine the nature of leaders' power in organizational environments, and it focuses on the ways in which leaders present themselves to others and motivate their followers in management settings.

In other words, this game is about the kind of interpersonal interactions that are most likely to result in the acquisition of power by leaders. Goffman (1975) writes about the presentation of self in everyday life; we think 'Behave Yourself' and 'The Photocopy Machine' help people to do just that — to present themselves more effectively as leaders in their everyday working lives.

'The Photocopy Machine' is useful for identifying whether individuals are primarily power-motivated, people-motivated, or task-motivated and how they will behave as leaders in each of these modes.

'The Photocopy Machine'

Everyone sits around a table and we tell them a story, which goes like this:

> 'The photocopy machine broke down in your office this morning and has only just been repaired. It is now 4:00 pm, and by 8:30 am tomorrow 150 folders have to be filled with 20 pages of material for a conference. It is your job as manager to tell your subordinate that he or she must stay late and do all the photocopying. You happen to know that your subordinate has tickets for a popular concert tonight, for which he or she stood in line for hours and to which he or she has been looking forward for weeks.'

Then we ask one person at the table to role-play the manager and someone else to play the subordinate. They take it from there. As in some of our previous descriptions of games, probably the best way to explain the purpose of playing 'The Photocopy Machine' is to share some reminiscences.

We remember one man, Jim, who played the manager. Jim started off by saying to his 'subordinate': 'Now, Tom, I'm not going to blame you. I know it wasn't your fault; it's just one of those things. It can't be helped.' Tom found himself replying: 'Well, thank you, Jim, I appreciate that', even though it was Jim's unfounded assumption that Tom was to blame in the first place. Jim continued: 'Don't worry about it. I know you'll get the job done, just like you always do. You're one of the most reliable people on my team, and I've got total faith in you. And I'll tell you what I'll do — I'll phone my wife and tell her 'I'll be late. I know she's got a dinner party and she'll be furious with me, but that can't be helped. I'll stay and help you for at least an hour.' Tom thanked him again with genuine gratitude and that was the end of the role-play. Not only did Tom have no opportunity to mention the concert tickets, he did not even want to mention them. His 'manager' had manipulated his feelings so successfully that he was willing, even eager, to do the job, and ended up thanking the manager for letting him do it.

At the end of a round of 'The Photocopy Machine', we usually ask the rest of the group: 'On the basis of what you've just seen and heard, do you think in this imaginary story that the conference delegates will have their folders?' On this occasion everyone felt that they would.

In another round of the game, with the same group but with different role-players, a woman called Esther played the manager and negotiated rather uneasily for a while with her 'employee', who became increasingly insubordinate. Esther stopped, looked at us, and said: 'I'm finding this really difficult, and quite untrue to life, because in my office this kind of thing just would not happen.' We asked why not, and she replied: 'Because the minute that photocopy machine broke down, I'd have been on the phone to the nearest printing firm to arrange for them to do all the conference material'. She maintained that crises never happened in her office (and she implied that they did not happen in her private life either).

'Funny', said Jim. 'In my office they happen all the time!' We asked if he ever precipitated a crisis, just for the intellectual stimulation, and before he could answer, his accountant (who was one of the group members) replied with feeling, 'Oh, yes!'. Esther was frankly incredulous; she just could not believe that anyone would want to behave in so irresponsible a fashion. Ordinarily, she would dismiss such a person as incompetent but she could not react that way to Jim, who was plainly very competent indeed. So then we were able to talk about what it feels like when someone who hates a crisis, who plans carefully and avoids crises, has to work with (or is married to) a person who thrives on crises and will apparently wantonly destabilize a situation or a relationship just because of a need for the creative stimulus of restabilizing it in a different way. Thus 'The Photocopy Machine' can increase real-life leadership skills in conflict handling and stress management by increasing people's knowledge of the ways in which they and others 'perform' so they can more effectively define and solve personal communication problems.

Another exercise that groups always find useful in studying personal performance is a role-play that we call 'Walk-On'. It must be videotaped because the object is for players to have a detailed observation of their own and others' body language, or non-verbal behaviour.

In the following version of 'Walk-On', the players focus on language, gesture, expressions, movements of head, body and limbs; to describe the game in general terms, the operators are put into simulations (not necessarily realistic) of situations requiring the real-life skill that they are to learn.

After a few rehearsals, the learners are videotaped. Afterwards the game director replays the tape to the whole group, stopping at appropriate moments to lead a short session of discussion and feedback. One advantage of this game-style teaching method for skills training is that it does not require the elaborate building of costly simulators because a cardboard cut-out is usually enough. The objectives are for students to gain an overview of the basic requirements of whatever it is, to acquire a sense of confidence through feelings of control of the process, and to benefit from the comments, advice and suggestions of their peers. The learning comes from a combination of a number of responses by the students as they go through four stages of an experiential cycle:

(1) First they have the *experience* of going through a series of activities.
(2) Then they *watch* their own performances in video replay.
(3) Next, they *reflect* on the results, and on the comments of a number of interested and sympathetic observers (who will themselves go through the same process).
(4) Finally, they *think* about ways to improve their abilities when they go on to more detailed instruction and practice in real life.

'Walk-On'

The game takes from one to two hours to play, depending on numbers, and is suitable for groups of six to 15 people, give or take a few. All you need is a room with plenty of space in the middle and a complete video recording system — that is, camera, microphone, recorder, and monitor for replay.

Divide the players into groups of three people and ask them, one group at a time, to walk into the 'performance area', ie the space in the middle of the room which is in the camera's range. Ask each person to carry a chair 'on stage', to put it down wherever he or she wants to inside the playing space (which you may have outlined with a chalk mark on the carpet, or encircled with chairs or something of the sort), and then to sit down on it. If there is no one around to operate the camera, it can be set up, switched on, focused on the playing area, and left to run itself. This has the advantage that on replay you can point out some general patterns of behaviour because everyone is on camera all the time; but the replay is more visually satisfying if there has been a camera operator to shoot close-ups as well.

Ask each group, when it goes on stage, to discuss a particular topic. We have found that most people do not respond well if you ask them to choose the topic. Usually you will reduce participants to embarrassed silence if you ask them, while they are very much aware of being on camera, to 'talk about whatever you like'. Depending on how well you know the group and what kind of response you are looking for, you can give them some general ideas. For example, you might suggest, 'Discuss why people vote Conservative'. Or more personal options may be suggested, such as, 'Find out why each of you dressed the way you did this morning'. Or you can request that the three discuss the merits of apartment living versus living in a house; or whether a staff canteen is preferable to having automatic food and drink machines in office buildings; or whether people should smoke in their workplaces. The list is endless and the choice of subject matter does not really matter. The object is to provide enough stimulus to get people talking without being too controversial (we have found it wiser to avoid topics concerning religion, race, or colour). Give each 'performance group' a different topic, and at least three minutes to talk about it. If you have only a few people, you can allow five minutes per group, but they really do not need more than that for your purposes.

When everyone has had a turn, gather round and watch the replay — which some participants will do with almost painful intensity. Then comment on the activity as if you were training everyone to be a professional theatre actor. We have found some of the great Russian director Stanislavsky's ideas about 'building a character' to be extremely useful in helping people to present themselves more effectively in their characters as managers in real-life roles. Stanislavsky (1962) suggests that a character is built in physical terms: body, voice, manner of speaking, walking, and moving; that these actions convey meaning to others — they are what he calls 'the inner pattern' of an actor's part.

We also follow two of the guidelines that the American director Tyrone Guthrie (1971) laid down for beginner actors. For example, these are some of the things that we look for when playing 'Walk-On':

(1) Many listeners signal in advance when they are about to speak, by some small sound, gesture, or movement while someone else is still talking. Guthrie advises actors, before they say or do anything on stage, to take a breath. He argues that the more deeply actors have to feel, the more deeply they must breathe. This breath must be taken not when they hear their cue, because then they will be late and create a meaningless pause, but 'when, probably from the previous speech of your partner, you get the idea that governs your own speech or reaction.'

When watching the replays, we can usually tell quite quickly that those who are most successful in 'taking the floor' are speakers who *time* their entry into the conversation. They inhale and make some slight movement just before they begin, and thus create a 'natural' pause as they catch the attention of the group, which they use to their own advantage. On one occasion when we pointed this out, some observers protested that one of the most effective speakers, who had moved in and out of his group's conversation with apparently effortless ease, had not physically moved at all. We replayed the tape and it did seem at first that this man had adopted a posture of great repose, sitting in a calm and relaxed way throughout his time 'on stage'. We played the tape one more time, with everyone crowding around the monitor and watching as closely as possible; we saw at last that he had the knack of taking a breath in exactly the way Guthrie describes. His speech flowed from an initial 'signalling' inhalation and thus followed the words of the previous speaker in smooth continuity. We asked this man (an engineer on a management course) if he was aware that this was his communication style. He replied that he had no idea of it and would try to forget it, in case he became self-conscious. However self-conscious people may feel when they first begin deliberately to study their body language, the increase in self-knowledge that they achieve should ultimately give them greater leadership power.

We usually point out, as part of the above observations, that if in 'real life' you are talking to someone and recognize 'I want to talk now' signals in your listener, there is no point in continuing to talk, even if you want to. The other person is not listening — all he or she is doing now is waiting for his or her chance to speak. And when you resume speaking after giving your conversation partner a reasonable amount of 'air time', you will probably have to recapitulate because your listener probably stopped listening for at least a few seconds before you stopped speaking.

(2) People's non-verbal behaviour can be recognized as a sequence of impressions. Observers can learn to anticipate and change the sequence of others' behaviour patterns. Guthrie argues that it is exactly this sequence of impressions that an actor must build up in order to achieve credibility in the role.

On one occasion, a woman positioned her chair so that she did not have to sit full face to the others but sideways, her hands tightly clasped in her lap and her body more than half turned away. She did not look at anyone even when she was directly addressed, and though she turned her head over her shoulder towards the speaker, she kept her body turned away. After a few moments' general conversation among the group, this participant felt confident enough to volunteer a comment, and as she did so, she automatically made several slight gestures with her hands. Her whole body began to look more relaxed and soon afterwards she turned directly to face the others, adjusting the position of her chair to move it closer to them.

Another woman in the same class (though not in the same group) began by placing herself almost out of camera range but ended by picking up her chair quite unselfconsciously and moving it right into the circle. When she watched herself doing

this on the tape replay, she was astonished. She had been aware
of moving the chair but had no idea how conspicuously she had
signalled, first her reluctance, and then her willingness to be part
of the group.

Power relationships can be studied in body language not only by
noticing where people place themselves in relation to others but
also how men and women behave towards each other. Once we all
watched while a man walked on stage in front of his two female
group members and placed his chair directly facing the camera so the
other 'actors' were virtually forced to sit with their backs to it. He
was thus both upstage and centre stage of the camera, which in the
theatre is the best position from which to command the attention of
the audience. His verbal behaviour added to his success at 'upstaging'
the others because he spoke clearly, even loudly, and sounded
confident. The other two players were both young women and he
appeared to take it for granted that they would defer to him, which
they did. (We talked later about how women are conditioned to
defer to men in leadership roles.)

When he had seen himself on the monitor in playback, we asked
him if he had been aware of all this. He replied that he had been
aware of how he was behaving: he had never seen himself on television before and was determined to make the most of the opportunity, even at the expense of his colleagues. This led to a discussion
about people's motives for doing things. If they want something
badly enough, they will behave forcefully in order to get it, which
indicates the importance of personal motivation and goal-setting for
leaders.

It is often the case that some people will achieve their objective
merely because they feel more strongly about it than their potential opponents and therefore their influence on followers is more
effective. If this behaviour is recognized as a sequence of impressions,
then it can be interrupted at a point most likely to throw the person
exhibiting the behaviour off balance. For example, if one of the
women had asked the camera-hogging man to move his chair, she
could more easily have prevented him later from stealing the show.
If she had recognized his initial behaviour as the beginning of a
pattern, she might have been more concerned about cutting it short.
However, in this case, the self-image of both women was so low that
they could only feel grateful for not having to face the camera,
even though doing so was the object of the exercise. One of them
had sat miserably hunched on her chair, with both arms tightly
wrapped round her breasts — a sure sign in women from Western-
type cultures of reluctance and anxiety (Westernized males tend in
such circumstances to put their knees close together and place their
hands together in their laps. When they feel more comfortable, they

usually spread their legs and let their open hands rest lightly on their knees).

'Walk-On' seems to be a game in which we can talk fairly freely about all of these things in a constructive way. We have always liked John Gielgud's definition of 'style' in acting as 'knowing what kind of a play you're in', and we quote this sometimes to players to illustrate the importance of appropriate behaviour for leaders; to help them recognize what 'kind of play' they are in, in any given leadership position in real life. They can then be more effective in sending out their own sequence of signals in order to gain control of the outcome — which is another way of saying that they can develop a leadership style.

Novelists and dramatists are aware that there are three stereotypes in stories and plays: the hero, the villain and the fool — though behaviour that is seen as heroic in one culture may be classed as villainous in another. The Japanese view suicide as an honorable act, for instance, but Christian societies condemn it. Leaders can be represented in fiction as heroes; like Robin Hood; or villains, like the plantation manager in *Uncle Tom's Cabin*; or fools, like the emperor who walked through the streets naked, thinking he was wearing new clothes. Readers, or audiences, will recognize them as such because of the behaviour patterns that their creators ascribe to them. Leaders in real life have to decide what relevant behaviour their supporters and others are likely to class as 'heroic' and then pattern themselves upon this.

Unfortunately, many people habitually transmit messages whose sequence builds up to a total impression of being, say, aggressive instead of assertive or pig-headed instead of strong-minded. They need to become aware of the cumulative effect of their behaviour on others so they can alter it when necessary. The following game illustrates the impact that such build-ups can have — while at the same time providing a thought-provoking example of the uses of power. There is a similar game, called 'Majors and Minors', in Joanne Hope's book, *Games Nurses Play* (Pergamon, 1986), but ours is a lot simpler.

'Them and Us'

This game of power and status requires the game leader to have control of a setting in which refreshments will be served at some time. We have played 'Them and Us' effectively during seminars held in hotels or conference rooms where the participants break for coffee or lunch by going to a specially prepared dining room. We ask the functions manager in advance to make the following arrangements for morning coffee:

(1) To group the chairs at one end of the room only.
(2) To set up two tables — one near the chairs with a big (preferably silver or fine china) coffee pot, cream jug, sugar bowl, cups and saucers, cloth table napkins, and plates of biscuits; the other one at the bare end of the room with nothing but a plain coffee urn and plastic cups.
(3) To label each table with a large, clear sign, one at the more heavily laden table reading 'US' and the other one at the more modest table reading 'THEM'.

The details will vary, of course, but the general effect must provide a sharp contrast in style and content between the two tables. Take the functions manager into your confidence, explain why you want the room to be set up this way, and say that you would like the waiters and waitresses to restrict their service to keeping up supplies. You will usually receive enthusiastic cooperation. We remember one waitress who became so interested in the results of the game that she asked us afterwards if she could give some feedback to the group, based on her observations of their behaviour. We were delighted to accept her offer, and the participants listened with great respect to her extremely pertinent comments.

Shortly before the coffee interval, explain to your participants that this will be a working break; then divide them into two groups. If you are working with multicultural, multilingual, or otherwise mixed participants, you may want to divide them into two homogeneous groups. Give each person a button or some other form of visible identification. All of the buttons for one group will bear the word 'US' and the buttons of the other group will read 'THEM' to define members of an in-group and an out-group respectively. Alternatively, you could use any other two words that relate more closely to your participants' real-life social or professional status (for example, 'OFFICERS' and 'OTHER RANKS'). Now distribute two sets of instructions, written on cards, one card to each participant. All of the cards for the 'US' group will read something like this:

'During the following coffee break you will find yourself among members of an 'in-group' and an 'out-group'. You are fortunate to be a member of the 'in-group', which means that you are one of 'US', not 'THEM'. You will recognize the others who share your exalted status by the 'US' pins that they wear. Please join them at the senior managers' table and sit in the comfortable chairs. If any of 'THEM' approach your table with a request of any kind, you will, of course, make sure that they behave respectfully or you will send them away.

The cards for the members of the 'THEM' group will read something like this:

During the coffee break you will all find yourselves to be members of either an 'in-group' or an 'out-group'. Unfortunately, you are one of the 'out-group', which is denoted by your button, which says 'THEM'. You may not take your refreshments from the table near the chairs — your table is the one in the corner. The chairs are reserved for the use of those whose buttons read 'US'; you may sit on the floor if you wish. If you should need anything from the 'US' table, you may go over and ask for it, but be sure that your manner is respectful and that you show by your behaviour that you understand the exalted status of 'US' people. If by any chance an 'US' person approaches your table, this is a great honour which you should acknowledge appropriately.

When the players go into the coffee room and become aware of the inequality of the situation, they react in a number of ways, some of them extreme. For example it becomes obvious very quickly to 'THEM' that if they want cream or sugar in their coffee, they are going to have to go over to the 'US' table and ask for it — which will mean either grovelling or risking a snub. If the first few tentative attempts are met with patronage by 'US' players, some 'THEM' people will not persist; they would rather take their coffee black or drink nothing at all than be a participant in an unequal interaction. This happened recently when we played this game at an international conference in France, at which papers and discussions were presented in French and English, but where power games were being played between the French-speaking and the English-speaking participants over which language would be used for informal conversations. Since France was the host country, we gave all of the French speakers the status of 'Les Francais'; the members of the out-group were 'LES AUTRES'. We specified that the only language 'LES FRANCAIS' would recognize in the coffee room would be French.

The French speakers were delighted with this chance to even up a few scores and behaved with a cool arrogance that 'LES AUTRES', especially the native English speakers, found annoying — so much so that none of them took any refreshment at all but stood around their table with their backs to 'LES FRANCAIS', talking in carefully non-modulated voices.

When we were all back in the conference room, the French speakers did not discuss their game behaviour at all, but kept the debriefing to an academic analysis of the value of games as learning strategies. The English speakers kept very quiet. We had no intention of forcing the issue, and were content to let the learning experience speak for itself.

Another example of an extreme reaction is when some players — Australians in particular — cannot handle the elitism of being 'US' and walk over to 'THEM' to make friendly conversation, only to become even more embarrassed when they are treated as visiting VIPs. On these occasions, we point out afterwards that in real life too, many liberal-minded Australians — and Americans — try to break down social and economic barriers by ignoring them, only to find that life is not that simple. British and Asian players tend to be much more pragmatic.

There are many different barriers that exist between people due to differences in cultural backgrounds, and there are many people whose leadership consists in finding ways to overcome these barriers. We have a game that is particularly suitable for studying ways in which cross-cultural misunderstandings can arise, and some possible ways to avoid or minimize them. It consists of four scenarios. Even though they are improvisations, as is 'Them and Us', they are much less open-ended because role instructions are given in much more detail. This enables game leaders to maintain a fair degree of control over participants' actions and reactions. We suggest, however, that you might need some cross-cultural experience before trying these particular examples. They were designed to help managers avoid some common communication pitfalls in multicultural environments. You can always make up your own rules, to make this game suitable for the particular communication problems your group members are likely to experience in real life.

'What Would You Do If...'

Select eight people, or ask for eight volunteers; form them into four pairs and give each member of each pair a copy of the relevant protagonist or antagonist role. Give them five minutes to read the material and prepare for the role. Allow them to ask you any questions about the roles. Then each pair takes it in turn to role-play their parts to the rest of the group, to be immediately followed each time by general discussion which is firmly but tactfully guided by you. This discussion is important because there are specific lessons that you want the participants to learn from each role-play; otherwise, you would not have constrained the roles in the ways that you did.

Role-Play 1: The Brochure

PROTAGONIST'S ROLE:
You have worked for five years for an organization that conducts business and government seminars for cross-cultural training. One of your editorial duties is to send out a quarterly brochure listing all of the programmes offered by your organization. A brochure was mailed out today and you have just noticed that you failed to announce an important seminar, which is to be conducted by a new employee whom you like very much. Your organization is expecting serious budget cuts and your colleague's job may be in danger if this seminar does not succeed. On the other hand, you know that there

has been some criticism of your own work and if this error came out, it might be your job that would be in danger.

ANTAGONIST'S ROLE:

Six months ago you started to work for an organization that conducts cross-cultural training courses for business and government people. Your work has been good but you are considered to be an 'ideas' person and an aide to others rather than a leader. You think there will be budget cuts in the near future, and unless you prove yourself to be a leader, you could lose your job. You have designed a seminar which received full support from your supervisors even though the cost to the participants was higher than usual. This means that advertising and promotion are of utmost importance. Today you received a copy of the quarterly brochure announcing all of your organization's programmes, but there is no mention of your seminar. You go to the person responsible for editing the brochure, who is in a slightly more senior position in the company than you.

In the general discussion after this improvisation, it is important to clarify the purpose of each of the characters. The objectives of the exercise are that the trainee playing the protagonist should practise how to express regret and make apologies, and how to give explanations in a tricky situation; the antagonist should practise how to make complaints effectively. The exercise is designed to demonstrate that all of these behaviours are culture-specific. For example, a Japanese protagonist might try to make amends by asking: 'What would you like me to do?' But if this is said to an American antagonist, fuel could be added to the fire because the American might answer: 'It's your job, not mine, so it's your responsibility to put things right.' Thus, your object is not to make value judgments about the 'best' way to behave to foreigners (and they to you) but to seek consensus from group members about the most appropriate way to negotiate the particular problem illustrated by the above scenario. Through the process of reaching consensus, the group members become more culturally sensitive.

Role-Play 2: I Don't Believe It

PROTAGONIST'S ROLE:

You are Korean. You have worked for IBM for about 15 years and have a good position in Korea as a local IBM manager. You are now in Japan on a technology transfer training project. You will be in Japan for one month and will then return to your own country to train Koreans in how to use this new machinery. Your instructor, a person who is very friendly and capable, and about your age, is from Singapore. You like Singaporeans in general and are impressed by their working style, but yesterday something happened which puzzles you. After the instructor had explained a rather complicated operation, he said: 'What do you think? Any questions?' You were really impressed that a machine could perform such a sophisticated procedure, and said: 'I don't believe it!' The instructor made no verbal response to your enthusiasm but later he asked to see you privately. You are going to see him now, but you are not sure why.

ANTAGONIST'S ROLE:

You are a Singaporean who has worked for IBM International for 15 years. You are responsible for a technology transfer project, in which you are training international IBM employees. After this training with you, the participants will return to work at IBM companies in their home countries. You have a good reputation among your colleagues for being honest, friendly, and capable. Yesterday something happened that upset you. After describing a rather technical operation with some new machinery, you asked: 'What do you think? Any questions?' A Korean trainee replied: 'I don't believe it!' You were angry at being told politely that you are a liar, and after the session you asked to see the trainee. Now you are about to meet with this Korean, who is about the same age as you, in an equivalent position with IBM, and with about the same number of years' experience. You want this person to know that you do not like being called a liar.

Cross-cultural communication theory suggests that the first thing both parties should do is to seek clarification of the other person's intended meaning. Therefore, the antagonist should find out exactly what the Korean meant by his or her remark. As soon as the Korean realizes that this innocent remark has been misinterpreted, he or she should explain how enthusiastic he or she really is about the new machinery, ie offer an explanation. If the dialogue is followed by a few compliments about what a good trainer the Korean thinks the Singaporean is, and what a good student the Singaporean thinks the Korean is, all should be well.

Role-Play 3: Meet the Wife

PROTAGONIST'S ROLE:

You are a Thai legal advisor to an American import/export firm in Bangkok. You are in your forties, married, and have four children. You were educated in Thailand and your foreign travel has been limited to driving to surrounding countries (Malaysia, Singapore, and a few years ago an attempt to go to Laos but the roads were too bad for your car). Automobiles and driving are your main interests. You bought a new Mazda recently for three times what it would cost in Japan. To prevent it from being stolen, you had a special alarm system installed which sends a signal to your office, your home, and a beeper which you carry with you at all times. Mostly you drive alone, though occasionally you invite a friend. Today you are attending a reception for the new American managing director of your firm. You have heard that his Corvette is being shipped from the States and you are eager to tell him of your interest in cars and about the new security system that you have for your car. Perhaps you can plan a trip together. You hope that there will be a chance someday for you to drive his Corvette.

ANTAGONIST'S ROLE:

A week ago you arrived in Bangkok to become managing director of an American import/export firm. You and your wife are staying in a hotel until your furniture and car (a Corvette) arrive next week. Today the firm has invited all employees to a reception in your honour. You are American, in your forties, married with two sons at universities in the United States. Your wife is an artist who in the last two years has had several exhibitions and won two outstanding awards. She is hoping to find a suitable studio and gallery in which to continue her work here. One of your sons is at Princeton University, majoring in international law. He has a very fine record and is vice-president of his class. The other son is studying American literature at Brown University, is editor of the student newspaper, and has sold one article to *Esquire* magazine. You are proud of your family and would like your staff to meet your wife soon, and your sons when they arrive for the Christmas holidays.

It appears here that the American needs to learn appropriate topics of conversation and the kind of small talk in which business people engage in Thailand, where family concerns are more private than in the United States. On the other hand, the Thai could do with some pointers on how to hint gracefully while making small talk.

Role-Play 4: The Company Pin

PROTAGONIST'S ROLE:

Before coming to Japan as an American office manager for a joint American-Japanese company, you did a lot of 'homework' in order to understand Japan, the Japanese, and their business practices. One of the things you learned was the obligations that exist both ways between company and employees. For example, Japanese workers are proud of their employers and take pride in wearing the company pin. Most companies require that it be worn during working hours, but many wear it all the time. At your office, you have noticed that a new secretary is not wearing her pin. When you asked her why, she said that she had not received it yet. You asked your personal secretary to see that she got one, and your secretary said that she would take care of it. Two days later, you saw that the new secretary was still not wearing the pin. This time she said that she would get it later. Wanting to show your understanding of Japan and your concern for the company, you got a pin and gave it to her. You are now about to meet the personnel director to check the background of your personal secretary, who seems not to be following your orders.

ANTAGONIST'S ROLE:

You are the Japanese personnel director for a joint Japanese-American company. An American office manager, recently arrived in Japan, noticed that one of his new secretaries was not wearing the company pin. He got a pin and told her to wear it whenever she was in the office. It is your duty to explain to him that the pins are not given to new employees until they have been with the company six weeks. Then the pins are presented during a small ceremony when the new employees are made 'family members'. Your job is to explain the situation to the foreign office manager in ways that he will find supportive, yet that will lead him to correct the mistake; and to explain why his personal secretary did not tell him about the ceremony.

In this case, the office manager's personal secretary would have felt it presumptuous to argue on her own initiative with her superior's commands, however inappropriate she felt them to be. The manager would have behaved more effectively if he had asked his personal secretary if she knew why the new secretary was not wearing a pin, before acting in an autonomous way that he should have known is quite uncharacteristic of Japanese companies.

This role-play offers a good illustration of the value to leaders of 'informants' within an organization — people who have worked there for some time, who know the ropes and can explain things to newcomers, if the newcomers have the sense to ask.

All of the above role-plays were designed to reveal particular areas of cross-cultural communication where we believe — on good evidence — that misunderstandings frequently arise. We think that we know some effective strategies to avoid these misunderstandings in the first place, or to clear them up if they do occur. One of the games we describe in the following chapter is a much longer simulation game, which takes virtually a whole day to play and which we also designed to explore cross-cultural conflict, but which offers useful suggestions for all leaders whatever the setting.

You will find that the debriefing of all of the following games focuses on task accomplishment rather than on people-skills, the focus of this chapter. Of course, this does not mean that interpersonal communication is not a vital element in task accomplishment, and if you want to play these games, you will obviously debrief them along lines that suit your teaching purposes. Our objective is to give you examples of a range of uses which games can be made to serve.

Chapter 6

Simulations

An excellent way to increase self-awareness for leadership is through simulation games. We describe them as 'simulation games' because they are task-oriented rather than relationship-oriented — though as we have said before, this is a rather artificial distinction. The relationships that develop between players as they work together to achieve a common task can become strong enough to tax the diplomacy of the most experienced game leader.

Since life in general seems to be getting more and more complicated, specialized and technological, it is not surprising that simulation games are following these trends. The latest fashion is for computer games in which the results of play are recorded in reams of print-out. Even when computers are not involved, we find that many simulations have been planned by their designers in such intricate detail that they take hours to set up and days to play.

Our simulation games are not like that. Even when we borrow ideas or formats from other gamers we prune them ruthlessly, keeping only the bare outlines and relying for effect on our methods of presentation and our experience in debriefing. We are trying to share these skills with you in this book. The following game examples are virtually no more than vehicles to convey a number of ideas about building a relationship between a game leader and a group of players in which the leader can function as a negotiator of meaning between the group and the material to be studied.

Thus in one respect our choice of games for this chapter was arbitrary. Whatever we might have included, the objective would have been the same: that you should have the opportunity to contemplate a number of different strategems for informing a group of people and motivating them to learn.

'Digicon'

'Digicon' is about leadership but it is also a good planning exercise. It takes from three-quarters of an hour to about an hour and a half to play and debrief, depending on numbers. It can be played with as few as four people and will still 'work', but its effects are much greater if there is competition between groups of players, and for that you need larger numbers, say eight people upwards. There is no top limit, providing you have plenty of space and can stand a lot of noise. You need no special materials, just ordinary classroom furniture. Each player should have a pencil and paper, and you must have a large door key, because this is the most important 'prop' in the game.

'Digicon' involves people playing the roles of either prisoners or robots (ie who behave as mechanical figures). There is one robot for every 'cell' of three to seven prisoners. Thus in a class of 12 learners there might be three robots and three cells, each holding three prisoners.

Make sure everyone has a pencil and paper, and then divide the players into groups of any number from four to about eight — the groups do not have to be the same size — and ask for one volunteer from each group to play a robot. Ask the robots to imagine that they are machine-made slaves who have to obey their masters. They can see, hear, move and respond like human beings, but cannot speak. Tell all the rest that they are prisoners locked in cells, and box each group into a corner or against a wall by pushing tables and chairs in front of them to represent their cells. Keep the cells as far apart as possible. The robots stand outside their respective masters' cells and await activation. Draw everyone's attention to a large door key that you have placed somewhere in the room in full sight.

Describe the following scenario to everyone. It will seem complicated when you read it but it takes only a few moments to explain and it seems difficult only on the first occasion that you direct the game. After that it gets easier each time, and you will find yourself adding all sorts of fancy touches.

The players are all characters in a science fiction story, either extra-terrestrial travellers (ETTs) or earth-bound robots. All the ETTs have been taken prisoner by earthlings and locked in cells. At any time they may be taken out by the guards and executed. Their only hope of escape is to order the robot slaves to bring them the key (which they can all see, wherever it is) which opens every cell door. But they have to be quick, because they do not know if the prisoners in the other cells are friends or enemies. If they escape first, they may release the others, or they may murder them.

The robots are free to move about anywhere except into the cells. Before the prisoners can use their respective robots they have to activate the robots' memory-banks by giving them a list of commands. The robots write these words down. However, they are not very good robots and their memories can hold only ten commands, each of not more than two words at the most. *These are the only sounds to which they will respond.* Moreover — and this is the really important bit — the command words cannot be in English or any recognizable language; they have to be nonsense-words like 'zin' for 'go forward' or 'chut' for 'go back'. If you want to be imaginative you can give the players a reason for this. You can say that each cell is full of multicultural prisoners who have no common language and therefore they have to make one up. The true reason will become obvious when the game is under way.

Each group of prisoners in each cell will have to decide what commands will mean what, and then put them into their respective robots' 'look-up table', so that when the robot is activated it can be ordered to go and get the key and bring it to the cell. Thus the robots respond to a list of predetermined commands. Once stored, these commands can be given in any order and used repetitively. *The stored lists in the robots' memories cannot be changed.*

When you have explained this, answer questions briefly, and make sure everyone understands what they have to do. Then give the prisoners five minutes to fill their robots' memory-banks. Each cell should begin discussing what words it will need to feed into its robot, and as the prisoners decide each of the commands, they and their robot should write it down, with the English translations. Keep checking to see that this is happening but do not interfere in any other way, and above all, do not offer any suggestions. If you are playing with a multinational group you will almost certainly find that at least one group uses command words from a real — if obscure — language that one of its members speaks, like Basque or Tamil. Allow this.

When the five minutes are up, send all the robots out of the room. Then announce that the guards have made some changes to the prison, and move the furniture around a bit — for instance, pull a table out into the middle of the room and explain that this is a tunnel that the robots will have to crawl through to get the key. Add some more obstacles, such as making it necessary for the robots to climb over something. You can move the key if you want to, and if you are playing 'Digicon' with a very clever group you can afford to be really sneaky and hide the key where the robots will not be able to see it easily.

By this time, some of the prisoners will be very dismayed, probably because it did not occur to them to commit to their robot's mechanical memory any words that meant 'crawl' or 'climb'. Reassure them and tell them to do the best they can. When all the prisoners understand the sequence of actions their robots must perform to get the key, recall all the robots and stand them all together against a wall. Take their memory sheets away and mix them up, then return them so that no robot has its original list. This will probably cause something like panic in both robots and masters, but explain that as the robots are only machines, it does not matter which of them responds to whose commands. Then announce that the robots are now activated and operational.

No one will know what to do at first, but sooner or later one or more prisoners will start calling out commands from their lists. The robots will each anxiously be scanning their own lists to find out what commands they contain, and what they mean. Eventually one of them will recognize a command and respond to it, which will clue the other players; and the race will be on.

There may be a lot of noise at this point, with everyone shouting out commands, insults and encouragement to the robots. If you have psyched the players into their roles, the robots will not cheat (much) and the prisoners will not walk out of their cells before they get the key. Under pressure and excitement the rules may get a little bent, so be on the watch to restrain the more enthusiastic players.

You may have to push people back behind the barricades, scan the relevant vocabularies if you think any robots are responding to more than ten command words, and forbid any command that sets one robot physically to attack another. We find that the safest thing is to say that if one robot touches another they both have to 'freeze' until their masters' commands separate them again. Remember this advice when you play 'Digicon' with young players.

You may need to use your own judgment about when to end the game, because even if one robot gets the key to one cell, the other prisoners may not notice it and may thus continue to direct their own robots. Even if they observe that the key has gone, they may still want their own robot to finish the course. The challenge of negotiating it through the various obstacles may be, for them, the most important part of the game.

On the other hand, some players may give up long before this point, because they know that their robot-vocabulary is inadequate. This decision is premature, as we know from experience that the most pitifully limited word-list can be stretched to an amazing extent by creative thinking.

Players usually find 'Digicon' great fun, and the thrill of the chase makes it a good warm-up game at the beginning of a conference. On one occasion when we did this, the successful prisoners ran around the room after their robot gave them the key, 'unlocking' all the other 'cell doors' in quite a ritualistic way. One of the rescued said later that this behaviour had probably been a critical factor in setting a cooperative standard for the conference as a whole. Robots often report that the process of being programmed makes them feel they 'belong' to the group that programs them; so it is a real 'culture shock' when they have to exchange vocabularies and discover themselves being directed by strangers. This comment is a good introduction to a discussion about the meaning and the power of organizational socialization.

Robots also develop strong opinions about who was 'really' in control during the game. Some robots argue that theirs was the real power, and they enjoyed it. When this happens we usually say, 'Surely all you did was obey orders?' However, they seem to feel that their masters would have been helpless if they had not interpreted the orders accurately. This can lead to an interesting debate about the division of labour in organizations — for example, whose is the real power, the people who give the orders or the people who have their hand on the switch?

Other robots respond differently — with feelings of helplessness and frustration. They describe how angry they became at what one man described as: '. . . an awful feeling, when you know that the people who have power over you are totally incompetent!'

The prisoners who escape first usually do so because they possess one of two dominant group characteristics. Either they have a strong emergent leader whose competence operates the robot with maximum efficiency, or they are very democratic and task-minded prisoners who take turns almost intuitively to contribute to the action in a kind of brainstorming process. In these latter groups, members clearly recognize and use each others' problem-solving strengths. For instance, there was one prisoner in a cell of three who remained silent while the others programmed the robot (she said she recognized that they were quicker than she at doing this and was happy to let them get on with it). She quickly proved so efficient at operating the robot afterwards that the others willingly fell silent and became satisfied observers of her performance in achieving their common purpose.

We think that as a learning strategy 'Digicon' fits very well into organizational communication programmes. For example, you can use it to study power relationships between management and workers within organizational settings; or the dynamics of task-oriented small groups, including leadership behaviour, under pressure from the environment. 'Digicon' is also effective in cross-cultural contexts, for instance, to promote understanding of different problem-solving styles between people of different national/ethnic/cultural backgrounds.

These suggestions are all derived from the kinds of response players make to 'Digicon', and their reactions provide some good general examples of how teams — with or without official leaders — solve problems and achieve tasks.

We play another game, called 'Gerontology', to induce a more specific kind of behaviour in the participants; and that is their response to the problems, personal and organizational, of growing old. Ours is a simplified version of a game of the same name in a book called *Australian Management Games* by Barry Moore. Though it was written some years ago (1978), it is still one of the best collections of management games that we know of.

'Gerontology'

This is a game that can have a stunning effect on groups of social workers, bank trainees, public health students and other managers who work in government departments, the private sector or non-government agencies which have to deal with the aged and the poor. Players might also be leaders of church associations or youth groups because so many people in the community, young as well as old, are concerned with the problems of senior citizens' health and welfare, whether they be neighbours, family members or friends.

'Gerontology' requires a large group of players — at least ten people and preferably more than 20, none of whom are very old. We do not think this is a good game for elderly people, as it is, perhaps, a bit close to home for them. Even youngsters sometimes get very depressed about the game's implications and you may have to talk them through these feelings. Like 'New Year's Eve Hat' following, 'Gerontology' needs really sensitive leadership. It takes at least two hours to play and debrief. Beforehand, assemble the following:

- Four small sheets of cardboard;
- Four felt-tipped pens, preferably in different colours;
- Lots of pencils and paper;
- Several boxes of paperclips;
- A ball of soft rope;
- A pair of scissors;
- About 20 cards, the size of playing cards, to contain messages from Death, who in this game is called the 'Grim Reaper'.

Cut the rope up in advance into a number of 1-foot lengths — at least three times as many pieces as you are going to have players. Write a number of phrases on the cards, repeating each phrase on several. Here are some examples: 'You have had a stroke and your brain is impaired. Give your pencil to the Grim Reaper'; 'You are very old and are losing your memory. Give your paper to the Grim Reaper'; 'You have to pay your phone bill. Give one paperclip to the Grim Reaper'; 'You have to buy a birthday present for your grandson. Give one paperclip to the Grim Reaper'; 'You have arthritis. Give one length of rope to the Grim Reaper'; 'Today you fell down and broke your hip. Give all your rope to the Grim Reaper'; 'You are dying. You have one minute to make a will if you wish, which the Grim Reaper will execute on your behalf. Then you must die, and leave the game to become a heavenly observer of the remaining players'.

When you have directed 'Gerontology' a few times you may want to write more of these Grim Reaper messages, or alter some of them. You may also want to give the 'heavenly observers' some written suggestions about the kinds of interaction they might usefully look for in the players who are 'left alive' — but do not worry about that yet because the above are sufficient for a first attempt.

You need access to the game room a few minutes before the players arrive because you first have to arrange their chairs in special rows. Allow one chair per person, and ten chairs to a row. Put most of them very close together with almost no room to move along the aisle between the rows. Arrange a few rows with chairs widely spaced with plenty of leg room. All the chairs represent residences. Some are in poor and overcrowded neighbourhoods while others are in salubrious suburbs with lots of space.

On each chair place at least one length of rope, a pencil, a sheet of paper and one paperclip. Put an extra piece of rope and two or even three paperclips on each of the widely-spaced chairs. Ropes represent players' mobility, paperclips their money, and paper and pencil their knowledge and experience.

At each end of the room there must be a desk and chair, with the chair behind the desk, facing out into the room. If there are more than 25 players and the room is large, set up four desks. They represent banks and welfare agencies. Try to arrange them so they are as far as possible from the rows of chairs. The bank should be close to the 'good' neighbourhood, and the welfare agency should be relatively near the poor quarter; but they both (or all) should be at least one rope's length away from the nearest chair in the nearest row.

On each desk put a sheet of cardboard, a felt-tipped pen, and (dividing out the supplies equally), the rest of the paperclips, pencils and papers. Put the remaining ropes *only* on the desk(s) of the bank manager(s).

When the players arrive, ask for two volunteers if you have a small group (say ten to 15 people), and four volunteers if the group is larger. Ask the volunteers to sit at the desks and tell them that you will visit them later with their instructions. Ask all the others to find a chair, gather up and hold the ropes, paperclips, pencils, and papers that are on it and then sit down, but not to change the position of the chairs. Ask them to tie one end of a length of rope to their wrist and another to the leg of their chair.

While they are doing this, go round to each of the volunteers. Tell those to whom you give the supply of ropes that they are bank managers. The ropes represent their clients' mobility, the paperclips are money, and the pencils and papers are for the managers to create any paperwork, special reference forms, etc, that they decide clients must complete before they borrow money. The ropes are for sale, for any number of paperclips each manager decides.

In order to negotiate with the bank, a client has to keep one hand on the manager's desk at all times. Tell the bank manager that this rule should be strictly enforced. A manager may wish to make other rules as well, such as insisting that the client makes an appointment, or shows identification, or whatever. The managers should interpret their roles as imaginatively as possible, and are free to act virtually as they want. Ask the managers to draw a sign on the cardboard with the felt-tipped pen, and prop it up on the desk, so customers will know the name of the bank, what the banking hours are, and so on.

Managers may leave their desks to visit anyone — for instance, the welfare agents — or just to take a break; but a responsible person must be delegated to 'mind the store' while they are away, and the bank will be closed to customers during that time. There is an imaginary telephone on the desk, so enquiries can be called out to anyone in the room, and information called back in return.

The other one or two volunteers are welfare agency representatives. They are to assess the needs of any client who visits the agency, and can give money at their discretion. The agency does not have any ropes, which can be purchased only from the bank. Give the agent(s) all the instructions that you gave the bank manager(s), and suggest that they may like to prepare some questionnaires, etc, for the clients to complete before aid is given; or they might want to devise some other form of investigation and/or selection process. Ask the agent(s) to use plenty of imagination in interpreting the role.

Now you address the room at large. You tell the group that they are all old people in the community. The chairs they are sitting on represent their homes, the paperclips their worldly wealth, the rope their mobility, the pencil and paper their knowledge and memory. At all times they must have one end of a rope tied to their wrists and the other end tied to the chair, but two or more lengths of rope can be joined together. The chairs cannot be moved but players may negotiate to buy each others' houses if they wish to move to another neighbourhood, or to acquire property for speculation. In these cases they can move to the appropriate chair, even if it means displacing its occupant. If this happens (say because an 'old person' has been forced by poverty to sell his or her home), the homeless one must sit on the floor, with the end of the rope caught underneath the nearest chair.

Apart from these provisos the players can do anything they want, provided there is not a rule that expressly forbids it. The people at the desks represent banks and welfare agencies, who are there to serve this community of senior citizens. They should be approached for advice and assistance when these are required.

Ask if anyone has any questions about what you have said so far. Repeat anything you have to. When everyone is silent, tell them that the game can now begin. Once the action is well under way, you should move quietly among the players. Your role is that of the Grim Reaper. Whenever you see anyone who appears to be rather too active — or for any other reason that seems good to you — give that person a card out of your pack. You may want to let players select one at random, or you may want to give them a specific handicap, or kill them off altogether, after which they have to leave the game and become observers.

We dislike this role very much because players quickly learn to greet the Grim Reaper with open dread, even hostility. We remember one man — a senior government employee — who shouted, 'Get away from me, you bitch!' when he saw one of us coming. It was unthinkable that he would speak like that to her in real life and after the game he was very apologetic. We reassured him that his reaction was a real tribute to the power of the game. All the same, we usually hand over the Grim Reaper role to the first player we decide should 'die' — which has the added advantage that it brings this person actively back into the game.

After you announce the beginning of the action, almost invariably people wait for you to tell them what to do next. You, however, pretend to be busy with the video camera or something, or you just sit there. Probably someone will ask eventually: 'What are we supposed to do now?' In which case you reply: 'How you play the game is entirely up to you. All I have done is set the scene for you; now you have to create the action.'

Sometimes they then call out to the bank manager, for instance, asking what they can do. The manager may mime a telephone call in order to reply that the client must personally visit the bank. People will begin to negotiate, to beg, borrow, or steal more paper clips and extra lengths of rope if they need them to reach the bank or the welfare agency. Gradually a society begins to emerge out of this collection of individuals.

It is up to you to assess the nature of that society. Is it individualistic or communal, capitalist or with some other form of economic structure? Within it, how are the old people treated and how do they behave towards each other? Are the bank and welfare agency very bureaucratic? Do people have to stand in line for government aid? Who gets rich and who stays poor? Why? You will find that the group dynamics are different depending on whether you allow a significant number of players to remain 'alive and well' long enough to get themselves organized and start having a good time. For instance, in one game we left players alone until several people found themselves 'jobs', like dusting people's chairs, and some others joined ropes together to make a community bus to visit housebound citizens. The bank manager was extremely obliging about overdrafts and the welfare agent dispensed paperclips on a regular basis.

Players' responses afterwards to a game like this are likely to be very positive. They will make statements to the effect that getting old is not all that bad, because there is always work to be found if you want it and anyway a community looks after its own.

On the other hand, if the game leader sees to it that the players gradually die, one by one, from various depressing illnesses and that those left behind find themselves wandering about aimlessly in an empty world with a great deal of money and mobility but no incentive to do anything, then the final reaction of the participants will be much more negative. It will occur to them to criticize the attitudes of society in real life that allow old people to wither away unnoticed and uncared for.

On one occasion a woman called Beth decided to 'commit suicide', ie leave the action and become an observer because, she said, she was 'starving to death' in her home. The Grim Reaper had struck her down, first with a severe illness so she had no mobility, and later with loss of memory so she had no paper and pencil. She had lent her sole remaining paperclip to a neighbour who had not returned it; in addition, the players in the chairs around her were busy chatting to each other, ignoring her. In the debriefing, Beth made it quite clear that she was still annoyed and hurt by the way her fellow players (in real life her fellow health administration graduate students) had treated her. For example, 'the woman next door' had acquired many lengths of rope but refused to give even one to Beth without payment even though it was obvious Beth could not afford to pay. Beth now asked this player: 'Why wouldn't you lend me even one rope, so I could move?' The woman, plainly disconcerted, replied that she had not wanted to restrict her .own mobility and added, 'Why are you taking this so seriously? It was only a game!' Beth answered: 'If it was only a game, why should it matter to you how many ropes you had?'

We think this is a good example of how scarcity of resources and constrained circumstances can put pressures on people to behave in antisocial ways.

These are the kinds of responses that make 'Gerontology' an effective problem-solving game in appropriate learning circumstances, but again it is one we recommend for experienced game-directors only. Its open-ended structure generates not only strong but very diverse and complex feelings. The next game does too.

'New Year's Eve Hat'

The object of this game is to find out whether there are any special attitudes held by and towards handicapped/disabled people in Western cultures — or, alternatively, to inform players that these attitudes exist, tell them what they are, and perhaps convey value judgements about them. The game takes one to two hours to play, and any number of people can join in, but it will not work very well with fewer than about eight. Materials must be provided so that every player can make a paper hat, but the makings can vary depending on budget. Basically, they should consist of:

(1) Sheets of coloured crepe paper bought from any stationery store;
(2) Scissors;
(3) A roll of cellophane tape, a small stapler and staples, and a packet of pins (at least one);
(4) A packet of balloons (uninflated), ribbons, etc, for decorating the hats if the game director can afford to supply these items. We have found that these decorative items greatly increase players' pleasure in their hats.

The represented situation is that a group of handicapped and non-handicapped people are going to make paper hats to wear in a fancy hat parade on New Year's Eve. The simulation consists of one participant playing a non-handicapped person for every five players who are 'handicapped'. The handicapped players really are disabled. Get someone to help you if necessary, and tie a player's thumbs, fingers, wrists, and arms together, and/or tie someone's hand behind his or her back, or a player's hand to a chair; and blindfold one or more players. The ties and blindfolds should be soft enough not to bruise the players, but strong enough to bind them. We find the best material to be (new) babies' nappies, folded diagonally. They are large enough for either binding or blindfolding. Other characters in the simulation are judges. If numbers are very small, there will probably be only one judge, but three judges provoke more controversy over judgement criteria. Describe the scenario with as much detail as your imagination can provide, stressing the social importance of the parade and the need for everyone to wear a beautiful hat (perhaps to impress the boss — a person's job may depend on it, for instance). Once the judge-roles are decided, the participants go into a huddle to decide their criteria. The more guidelines you give the judges the more specific will be their value judgements about the hats, and some of the game's options will begin to close up.

Thus at this early stage of the game it is within your control to keep the structure of the game open or to constrain the players within particular assumptions. Your decision will depend on what you want the players to 'know' at the end of the game that they did not know before. For example, if you have a group of managers who work in the advertising industry, and you want them to become more aware of the commercial constraints under which they work and which limit their leadership power, then you might give the New Year's Eve Hat judges a list of criteria that emphasizes the saleability of the hats and makes no allowance for the handicaps of the makers. On the other hand, you might want a group of social workers to get a gut-level experience of the kind of social discrimination that handicapped people receive. In that case, you could give some of the hat-makers more colourful materials than the others, then make 'colourfulness' one of the judgement criteria, and ask the disadvantaged players afterwards how they felt. Another strategy you might want to try is to give a pair of children's blunt-tipped scissors to the 'blind' hat-makers. Then when you debrief the whole exercise, you can point out that the ways in which society protects its handicapped mambers from injury sometimes also increases their handicaps.

In any event, when the game starts and the judges are discussing their roles, put the hat-makers at one large table or separate tables, and make sure that four out of five players are handicapped in any one group. Either the hat-makers are each given their own materials or there is a communal supply. If you provide communal hat-making materials, you force the players to share resources; then afterwards you can comment on how this was done, ie who was advantaged and who was disadvantaged even further in the process. Time the hat-making process carefully, giving players not more than 15 minutes at the most; ten minutes is usually enough. Then the hat parade takes place with all the competitors parading past the judges in their hats (make a note of details at this point, such as, how did the blind people handle the situation? Did anyone offer to guide them? If so, what happened? If not, why not? And how did the people manage who were tied to their chairs? Then the judges give their verdict and the game is over. If the judges take forever to make up their minds — and they often do — then allow the blind players to take off their blindfolds so they can see the hats and generally feel that they are part of the action again. But point out afterwards that in real life people are often so eager to be 'fair' to handicapped people in the community that they add to their burdens — such as making them wait around in very uncomfortable conditions.

One time when we played this game, a badly handicapped man and a non-handicapped woman collaborated so effectively to make their hats (she gave physical assistance, he advised about design) that their partnership became a joint entry in the competition — they created the headgear of a bride and groom. This was in stark contrast to the behaviour of a young woman, slightly handicapped, who became the protector of an older male player who was 'blind'. Her attitude was so maternal that he found himself acting like a child, finally demanding loudly to be taken to the toilet in the middle of the hat parade. Another woman refused all help, even though her hat collapsed just before the parade and she had to struggle slowly and painfully to remake it. A non-handicapped man neither offered help nor was asked for help by anyone. He worked in isolation, made a hat, then announced that he would take part in the parade 'just for fun', not as a competitor. All these actions provoked heated discussion when the game was over. For example, one man strongly criticized the independent behaviour of the handicapped woman who had insisted on making her hat all by herself. He said: 'If it takes you half an hour to tie your shoelace, then it's better to let someone else do it for you, so you can spend your time inventing a better mousetrap.' Everyone resented the 'patronizing' attitude of the non-handicapped man who did not want his hat judged with the others. This astonished him, for he had genuinely thought his action was right and just. And one seriously handicapped woman (she could not use one hand at all, and did not have the use of the thumb on the other) was frankly furious at the judges. They had ranked the handicaps in order of disability and marked the owners' hats up or down accordingly. The woman said: 'How dare you people, who have no handicaps, sit in judgement about whether it is "worse" to be blind or maimed?' One of the judges was so upset by this that he turned on us and blamed us for 'making' him act as a judge. He said that he deliberately avoided judgement roles in real life, that he had not wanted to be a judge in the game, and that he felt betrayed that we, via the game, had seduced him into uncharacteristic and humiliating behaviour. The whole group talked about its feelings for more than two hours after this particular game session, and members were still arguing, in twos and threes, as they went to dinner (it was a residential course). It is worth remembering that, as a general rule, a highly experiential simulation game will take twice as long to debrief as it will to play. (Our debriefing on this occasion concerned itself with the division of labour in organizations and in society, the nature of personal handicaps, and the ethics of judgements.)

It is important for teachers and trainers to be aware that many players respond with anger and hostility to highly experiential games. This is because such exercises often provoke action by some of the participants that may run counter to others' most deeply cherished beliefs and values. The argument for these controversial games is that leadership — and, therefore, leadership training — is not always a comfortable task. Self-questioning is an integral part of it, as is the ability to assess where others are likely to stand on any given issue, and the development of a broad perspective that can accommodate many views of the same situation. Nevertheless, these are not games for beginners to direct.

Now for a much easier problem-solving game, based on an unpublished article (as far as we know) by B W Neville and R S Hubbard, called 'The Multi-Purpose, Multi-Phasic Building Blocks Game'. Neville and Hubbard applied the concept of 'Broken Squares' (which we described in Chapter One) to invent the game. Apparently it had its origins in an attempt to design a simple exercise to demonstrate some of the barriers to communication which come from people's belief that their 'reality' is the same as that of everybody else. As they say, 'while each of us sees our behaviour as an appropriate response to reality, we are inclined to see the behaviour of those who thwart us or criticize us as stupid, irrational or malicious.' The authors assumed that an exercise which simulated this conflict of perceptions would be a useful training device. Their game is very good but very complicated and requires more than 30 players. They suggest a simplified version, and this is the one we have adapted as a simulation to encourage players to think about the factors that promote team-building and those that deter it.

'Infernal Towers'

Divide your group into teams of six people. Give each team a large quantity of Lego or similar interlocking building bricks. Give each member of each team a card bearing a specific piece of information regarding the task, as follows:

(1) The tower must contain 20 blocks.
(2) The tower must be ten levels high.
(3) The tower must be built of white, red and yellow blocks only.
(4) The tower must be built of blue and yellow bricks only.
(5) The sixth level of the tower must be a different colour from the rest.
(6) It is your task to build the tower. If other members of your team try to handle the bricks you must stop them and insist on doing all the actual building yourself.

If for any reason you want to have more or less than six people on each team, you can vary the number of instruction cards. Feel free to make your own instruction cards. The only criterion is that the respective instructions must be conflicting.

When you first assemble the teams, explain that they have to build a tower with the Lego bricks (or their equivalent) and hand out the instruction cards, one to each player, adding that no one else is to know this information. Announce that the game will be played in silence, and let them get on with it.

'Infernal Towers' is fun to watch (video it if you can) because of the evident confusion, bewilderment and frustration of individual players as they attempt to carry out their instructions only to find themselves obstructed by the behaviour of their team members. Expectations are confounded right, left and centre as people begin by assuming that they are all working together on a common task only to discover that they seem to be doing no such thing.

We recorded one playing of 'Infernal Towers' in a television studio for an educational television programme and the camera operators were all laughing at the action. Anybody who has ever had anything to do with television camera operators will know that they are the hardest people in the world to impress, so we chalked up another 'plus' for the game.

Some examples of things that are likely to happen are that one player attempts to place a blue brick, only to have it removed, with apparent indignation, by another player. A third will try to stop anybody else from doing anything, and so on. One of a number of situations tends to repeat itself from game to game, and we use this afterwards to initiate discussion:

(1) The player who is instructed to be the sole builder succeeds in being so. This happens when a forceful person is given the role, one who is effective in body language and who makes it plain that he or she will brook no opposition. Under these circumstances the other team-members sit back, more or less patiently, depending on their individual temperaments, and watch the self-designated builder. All goes well until he or she does something contrary to another player's instructions. Then this player gives silent protest and usually the builder heeds it and alters the design accordingly. When two protestors are in conflict with one another (perhaps because one wants no red or blue bricks) the builder often experiments by trying one brick after another until both protestors indicate that they are satisfied — for instance, when the yellow bricks are used exclusively. This team behaviour often works very well and when there are several teams, a group such as the above will usually be the first to complete their tower to the required specifications and will feel very pleased with their performance, and each other. This is probably because nobody has lost face. The initial humiliation felt by team-members at not

being allowed to touch the bricks is overcome by the builder later heeding their instructions as to how it should be built. We have discussed previously the concept that leadership is a trade-off between leader and followers.

(2) The self-designated builder is overcome by powerful opposition from other players who insist on handling the bricks. This behaviour usually leads to a considerable amount of conflict. We have known people use force to snatch bricks from each or to remove bricks already laid. When things develop this way, it is unlikely that the tower will be completed.

(3) There is a combination of the above strategies. A time-consuming process of negotiation takes place between would-be builders which continues throughout the construction. Every brick becomes the subject of non-verbal debate, sometimes heated. Given time, the tower will eventually arise but a team which behaves like this will not win the game against one which adopts strategy (1).

It should now be obvious why 'Infernal Towers' is such an effective exercise for studying the behaviour of teams in real life. Another team game, which is much more commercial, is 'Model Aeroplanes'. There is a much more elaborate version in *Organizational Psychology:* Kolb, Rubin and MacIntyre (1984), but you will find that ours is every bit as good as theirs for a comparative study of team efficiency.

'Model Aeroplanes'

This will take at least two hours to play, so if you are not sure you will have that much time, do not play it. The discussion afterwards is the real learning experience and it must not be cut short because so many interesting ideas and observations come out of it.

Form all the players except two (or more than two if group numbers are large) into teams of five to seven people each. Tell them that each team represents an aircraft manufacturing company whose business is to make and sell model aeroplanes, which will have to pass a quality control test (ie they must fly) before a government purchasing officer will agree to buy them. Ask each company to give itself a name, which you post.

Each team has to choose a general manager (GM) to be in charge of purchases and production; and an assistant general manager (AGM), who is responsible for quality control and sales. The other team-members are assembly-line workers.

Now introduce the two people you have kept in reserve as, respectively, a purchasing officer (PO) and a quality control manager

(QCM). The QCM has to test the model aeroplanes, and those that pass are handed on to the PO for purchase. Paper sheets with which to make the aeroplanes can be bought from the PO at 10 pence a sheet, and the aeroplanes (which can be made from a single sheet) will be purchased for 15 pence each, providing they pass quality control.

Remember to come to this game well supplied with paper — you will be surprised sometimes at how much is used. You can devise a price list if you want to (Kolb, Rubin, and MacIntyre's lists need an accountant to understand them). If you are lucky enough to have an economic expert to play the role of PO, so much the better; ask that person to work out a discount price for bulk orders of paper, or any other refinement he or she cares to invent. However, this is not really necessary. For your purposes you can afford to keep the game as simple as we describe it.

Give everybody half an hour to play the game. You can issue a standard model aeroplane design, if you like, which everybody has to follow, or you can say that any design will do, providing the planes will fly (how 'fly' is interpreted depends on the QCM. This game leaves a lot of responsibility to the players). Note that if you insist on a standard design, some teams will negotiate with the PO to accept another one. Whether or not this strategy is successful will depend on the PO. We think the game works better this way because it stretches the players more, but the process will take longer than if you leave the design open.

Having set the whole thing up, you can afford to relax for half an hour and amuse yourself by watching the show. Sometimes the air becomes so thick with flying aeroplanes that you have to watch out that you do not get one in the eye. Frequently the assembly line workers spend as much time in testing their planes as they do in making them.

Eventually you collect everybody's attention (which may be difficult) and post the results. One team will emerge as the winner as far as profit is concerned but the really interesting part is in discovering how the various team dynamics worked and how the companies ran their businesses. Government employees are often made very thoughtful by this game because they are not used to working to an economic bottom line (which tells us something about criteria for public expenditure) and it gives them valuable insights into private sector thinking.

Some companies will not hesitate to cheat, for example, by forging the QCM's signature to get a faulty plane accepted by the PO. When this happens, we like to start a discussion about business ethics. Profitability seems to depend, in most playings of the game, on good design rather than careful construction (we do not know what you want to make of this), and time and again a team-member will come up with a brilliant design that wipes the floor with all competitors.

All in all, 'Model Aeroplanes' is rich in human potential. When we played it on one occasion on the first day of an intensive residential course for senior government officials, the course organizer told us later that it provided a benchmark for everything that came later.

The last game in this chapter, which we call 'Talking Heads', is a simulation of management problem-solving in international business. Unlike games such as 'New Year's Eve Hat' or 'Gerontology', it has a tight structure with detailed roles and rules. One of the reasons we have left it till last is that its description illustrates — perhaps more clearly than any other game in this book — how the leadership style of the game director influences the course of events. It is by way of prelude to our next chapter, about directing and debriefing games.

'Talking Heads'

Reorganizing for Greater International Productivity

The purpose of this game is to make players more aware of a range of important factors that affect the conduct of a business meeting involving people of different cultures. Virtually any number of players can take part because, if the roles run out, the remaining participants can be observers and their information can be used as feedback to the players at the end of each session.

The game takes most of one day to play and the debriefing runs throughout the game instead of being restricted to the end, which has the effect of breaking the action up into sessions. This arrangement enables you to maintain control of the simulation by the simple device of stopping the game every 20 to 30 minutes in order to comment on the players' behaviour.

Perhaps surprisingly, these artificial and periodic interruptions — rather like the commercial breaks in a television programme — do not seem to affect players' concentration when they resume their roles. Nevertheless, you should be aware that your 'interference' will to some extent (more or less, depending on the group you are working with) impose your value judgments on the game. Thus when the action starts again you will have given the players a push towards particular kinds of behaviour. Therefore, you want to be sure that this is the way you want the action to go — which implies that you should be well informed on the subject of international and intercultural business negotiation before you direct this game.

The participants have two tasks:

(1) To make recommendations concerning proposed changes for an imaginary company called Saito Corporation;
(2) To recommend a single corporate language for Saito Corporation's international dealings.

They are required to adopt certain positions, which are outlined on cue cards they receive at the beginning of the game (we describe them in the Appendix beginning on p. 167 because they would take up too much space here). These roles may or may not accord with opinions held by the role-takers but nevertheless it will be their task to argue in support of them as effectively as they can. In addition to the individual role instructions, all players are given the same general scenario, which we summarize here so that you can make sense of the game:

- In 1950 Saito Corporation, a petrochemical company, had an export department which took care of its foreign business, which was only about 7 per cent of its total. However, in the 1960s, Saito began to make major foreign investments and in 1965 the company was restructured according to geographical region. Today all country managers outside Japan report to and are supervised by an international vice president. Each country is managed largely with local staff. Company reports and all international mail are written in the local language with a translation in Japanese. Further market expansion has now led to the creation of more divisions within the international section, more and more involved with one another, and much confusion has resulted.
- The President and Board of Directors are now considering a proposal for an organizational restructuring. Under this new plan it is suggested there be five vice presidents: one each for North America, South America, Europe, Asia, and Japan. All of the individual national divisions are to be directed by managers who will report directly to their respective vice president. The goal of the reorganization is to coordinate production and marketing efforts across the entire corporation. Furthermore, many company leaders believe that a single language must be chosen as the international language of Saito if that goal is to be achieved.
- In the roles of national division managers the players are invited to meet with each other in order to decide on this international language for Saito and to review the proposed organizational changes for the company. The scenario specifies that recommendations made by this group will be sent to Saito's President and Board of Directors, and are likely to be followed.

All of the above may seem very complicated, but you will find that any group of managers grasps the essentials very quickly, and individuals seem to have no difficulty in assuming their roles as the respective national managers for Korea, Thailand, the Philippines, Singapore, the Netherlands, France, India, the United States, Brazil, Great Britain, Taiwan, West Germany, and Italy (if you have fewer players you have fewer roles. Pick the ones you like best). Basically what the players have to do is sit around the 'conference table', ostensibly to discuss the ramifications of the proposed organizational changes to Saito Corporation and to decide on a single international language for all its future negotiations. However, all the delegates have hidden agendas as well, because you can tell from the game setting that they will all have strong vested interests in both the organizational structure and the official language of Saito's huge international branch.

For example, the manager from Korea wants the international arm of Saito to drop its attachment to Japan and the Japanese language, which Koreans do not like, and to adopt English as its international language. The manager from Thailand is not really interested in either of the conference objectives, but is far more concerned to bring up more important matters, such as his or her personal problems in managing cultural differences.

The representative from the Philippines is a Japanese national, since no local Filipino has yet been found who is qualified to be manager. Therefore this representative wants Japanese to be the company's official international language; and likes the proposed reorganization of Saito's international branch since it will make him or her a manager, and if he or she does a good job he or she will get back to the home office in Tokyo.

On the other hand, the manager from Singapore thinks the proposed reorganization plan is far too complicated and will cause more problems than it tries to solve; and English has got to be Saito's international language because, even though Singapore has four official languages (Malay, Tamil, Mandarin and English), everybody knows that English is *the* international language of business... And so it goes on. Everybody has some sort of personal stake in the outcome of the conference, and the unfortunate chairperson has to try and get all of the participants to some form of consensus on the two agenda items.

As game leader, your role is to hold a watching brief and halt the debate at what you decide are critical moments. This requires a high degree of concentration and, as we have said before, considerable experience of international negotiation. This does not have to be direct experience. You may be a university lecturer, a director of international training programmes, an expert in teaching English as an international language, an organizational orientations manager, or some variant of any of these positions.

These are some of the things you need to consider when you are deciding whether to interfere with the behaviour of the players during 'Talking Heads':

(1) The emergence of 'hidden agendas'.
(2) Whether you should add extra information from your own knowledge, perhaps about the cultural imperatives of the represented nations.
(3) What strategies are being employed by the chairperson to achieve consensus and whether, in your opinion, they are working.
(4) The chairperson's management of time.

You may have to interfere with the game's 'real time'. That is, you may decide to ask the players to assume that a certain stage has been reached in the negotiation, even if it has not. For instance, you might feel that discussion has gone on long enough over Item 1 of the agenda, the proposed reorganization of the company. In that case, do not hesitate to move the players on by restating the scenario to include an imaginary vote by the players on this motion, which has been passed or rejected, and therefore the players can now proceed to debate Item 2.

You may meet with opposition from one or more of the players against your authoritarian handling of the game. This is all to the good because the objections will increase players' commitment to the game. Remember that people are likely to make a fuss about something only if the matter is important to them. Therefore, hear them out and be prepared to submit to their point of view if it seems reasonable.

During one playing of the game, the player who had the role of the manager from Thailand became really obstructive. You will remember that this role has the hidden agenda that cross-cultural communication problems shall be discussed at the meeting even though the topic is not part of the official proceedings. The man who assumed the role was so determined to adhere to it that the conference at one point came virtually to a standstill because the chairwoman did not seem able to handle the disruption. Yet in real life she was a senior manager who presumably was more than capable of such a task. We needed to clear the bottleneck, so we stopped the action and asked this woman what she would do if the situation was real. This freed both her and the 'manager' to discuss their feelings. He was mildly resentful of our interference and insisted that his behaviour was in keeping with his role. Having clarified this, we allowed the dramatic action to continue but the chairwoman, now forearmed by the realization of what she was up against, was able to deal much more firmly with the situation, and the business of the meeting continued.

The roles are gender-free and have no names assigned to them, though players will probably want to invent names that are appropriate. The main objective of the game is to promote greater cross-cultural sensitivity in the participants, no matter what the culture. Therefore the roles are not cultural stereotypes; they focus on general issues for leaders in international settings. Players never seem to find it difficult to assume the role of another nationality than their own, but sometimes we find ourselves involved in a discussion of role-playing in general. Maybe this topic is a good one with which to end this chapter.

We have always adopted the view that nobody can 'be' anybody else, not even professional actors. If a man plays the part of Othello, he does not have to be a real-life murderer. He calls on those emotions and feelings common to all of us that, taken to extremes, could theoretically end in murder. Thus in effect he plays himself (or a part of himself) in a simulated scenario. When real-life students or business people are asked to play a simulation game, and to assume a role with a name and a background different from their own, they are not being asked to be other than themselves. They are asked to follow the 'script' and the rules and to interpret them from their total life experience, direct and indirect, of the real world. Simulation games are no more and no less than their name implies. The participants put themselves under the general guidance of a game leader, assume an imaginary situation or event, behave as they would if it was real, and observe the consequences.

Our final chapter discusses the behaviour and attitudes, not of players of games, but of real-life participants who throughout life must assume different roles.

Chapter 7

Directing, Debriefing and Evaluating Games

This is the chapter in which we pull together the threads we have drawn so far and try to weave them into a coherent pattern. We hope that by this time it has become apparent that we believe the content of a game — ie the meanings ascribed to it by its players — is dependent partly on the form in which it is presented to them. In other words, in gaming as in any other communication process, the medium is an important part of the message.

Moreover, we think that this statement provides the vital clue which explains why gaming is often such a risky business and why evidence for its effectiveness is so hard to come by. Anybody who has researched the literature of simulation games will be aware of the controversy that bedevils them, even after decades of use in all kinds of learning environments. Enthusiasts are convinced that in some circumstances, and for some forms of learning, gaming can be a more powerful and economic strategy than any other. On the other hand, critics argue that gaming is always of doubtful value because its results are impossible to evaluate, can sometimes be counterproductive to learning, and in any case, is unnecessarily time-consuming. Between these two extremes fall many teachers and trainers who would like to 'give gaming a go' but are unable to find suitable games or adequate briefing.

The implicit message of our book has been: 'It's not only the game but what you do with it that counts.' Now we want to explain this more precisely. We think there are three factors that you need to take into account when you look for a game to direct with a group of learners:

(1) What you want the learners to get out of it.
(2) The form or structure of the game design.
(3) The character and temperament of your group of players.

We will illustrate what we mean by relating some 'typical' stories of how experienced teachers have used three games described in this book: 'Digicon', 'New Year's Eve Hat', and 'Gerontology'. We will describe how they adapted these games to suit their particular needs and how they debriefed them more or less effectively depending on their assessment of the players. We acquired this information as part of a research project in which we asked 35 educators to act as our informants. Between them they played all the games in this book and recorded both play and debriefing on audiocassette.

On the basis of this research — of which the following anecdotes are examples — and our own observations over the years, we have drawn up a table of generalizations and designed an 'evaluation game' to help game leaders refine their strategies. We give these to you in order to encourage you to join our research so that you can support or refute our suggestions from your own experience of playing games.

Our first example concerns 'Digicon'. As you will remember, its setting is that of a prison in which teams of players impersonate groups of prisoners locked in separate cells. Their only hope of getting the key and escaping is to give commands in an invented language to human 'robots'. The following are some of our assumptions about the structure of the game and the effects this structure seems likely to have on its players, depending on the leadership behaviour of the director and the composition of the learning group. We stress that our remarks are only suggestions and we offer them in a spirit of debate rather than instruction.

(1) 'Digicon's' scenario is established by a narrative device. A story is told about prisoners and robots that begins before the start of the game action. This use of narrative appears to have two results:
   (a) All the players tend to begin the game with similar feelings about it — usually a certain amount of excitement and suspense. Thus some degree of consensus seems to become established in the group of players before they start playing, which appears to predispose them — even if mildly — to receive the same kinds of learning messages from the game.
   (b) The nature of the roles is defined before the game begins, which inclines the players to see the roles the same way, and tends to restrict their interpretations to the pre-set parameters. This is another aspect of the game that seems to promote group consensus.

(2) The game requires players to be in small teams and the action includes rules that can be strictly enforced. These factors increase the game leader's control over the group's activities.

(3) There is a logical and regular sequence of events, also under the leader's control.

(4) 'Digicon' is task-oriented and the actions and reactions of the players are constrained within an ever-narrowing focus as the robots near completion of the task. These characteristics seem to have the result that the players become more interested in

how the game ends than in exploring their own possibly conflicting feelings about what has been happening in the game.
Thus, they tend as a group to be less critical than they might
otherwise be — and less likely to question any assumptions the
game leader may afterwards want to make on the basis of their
behaviour.

All of these factors seem to work towards convergence. That is, the
players, as a group, may be inclined to come to similar conclusions
about what the game 'means' when applied to real life.

This implies that if you want to use a game as a means of instruction — perhaps to demonstrate a particular theory such as Fiedler's
theory about the dynamics of leader/task/followers interaction
(Fiedler and Chemers, 1974) — then games that have a consensual
(or 'closed') structure similar to that of 'Digicon' will probably be
suitable for your purpose. However, the composition of the playing
group must be taken into consideration. Therefore, this tendency
that some games seem to have towards convergence will be less
marked if the group is made up of individuals who:

(1) Already hold strong views about the subject matter the game is
being used to illustrate.
(2) Are in some other way motivated to question any assumptions
the game leader might make about what happened in the game.
(3) Are highly pragmatic or empirically-minded people (such as
statisticians) who are unaccustomed to learning through analogies
or metaphors — which is what games are.

Nevertheless, the leader is the third critical variable in this game-
group-goal process. If it is true that 'messages' are conveyed to
players through the ways in which a game is organized and presented,
then presumably if the leader wants players to agree in general about
what the game 'means', he or she can make the task easier by altering
its structure — as the following example shows.

Peter directed 'Digicon' at a university drama conference attended
by drama teachers from all over the state. He wanted his players to
become favourably aware of the advantages for drama teachers and
students in taking an 'ensemble' approach to staging school plays
(which means that theatre director and cast should work demo-
cratically to build the show). Therefore he needed to demonstrate, in
game form, the advantages of close collaboration between members
of a team and their leader, in a democratic atmosphere of mutal trust
and confidence, to achieve a common goal through planned division
of labour.

Peter had previously asked us to recommend a game for him to use
at the conference, and we suggested 'Digicon' because we thought
drama people would have a lot of fun with such a dramatic scenario.

Also it seemed suitable because Peter's objectives were judgemental (he wanted the group to perceive the advantages of ensemble productions). He needed to create a spirit of consensus in his players, especially since they were all experienced professional teachers, drama-trained, independent-minded, imaginative people who would be likely to 'do their own thing' with the game if they were let loose, and who presumably already held fairly strong ideas about how to direct student theatre.

Peter made some changes to our original design of 'Digicon', but when we asked him why, he was unable to say more than that they 'felt right' to him. He is a very experienced teacher and his professional instincts support our theory about the form of a game influencing its content — because what he did, in effect, was to enhance even further 'Digicon's consensus-making characteristics:

(1) He allowed no talking at all except for the robots' non-English command words, which had to be conveyed to their memory lists by mime. This heightened the communication barriers between prisoners and robots. Their efforts to overcome these barriers turned them into a very cohesive group — which worked to Peter's advantage in debriefing, when he wanted them to reach a consensus (that ensemble productions are 'a good thing'). If group members are like-minded, a leader needs only to convince one of them and the rest are likely to follow.
(2) He allowed each robot to stay with its original cell of prisoners, instead of changing over the respective vocabulary lists. This had the effect of 'binding' robots emotionally more closely to their commanders and further enhancing team spirit.
(3) He created some extra roles, those of jailers, to enforce the rules. He privately briefed these actors to wander round the room during the play, ensuring that nobody left their cells and the robots did not cheat, thus increasing by delegation his own control over the action.
(4) He presented the game as a problem-solving exercise in which everybody could win rather than as a competition between opposing forces — another consensus-making device.

The result of all this was that though the players became very excited and involved in the game with a great deal of noisy activity, particularly towards the end, their apparent spontaneity was all the time being guided in ways that suited Peter's ends.

In debriefing he was quick to follow up any comments the players made that furthered his purpose. He began by asking: 'Did you enjoy the game?' — the first of many consensus-making questions. Immediately players began to comment on what fun it had been, praising it for generating a good group dynamic and 'getting [the conference] off to a flying start'. Peter asked for examples and one of the robots replied that the cooperation between her and her team to create her memory-list had caused her to feel that she 'belonged' to her team-members. It became very important to her 'not to let them down' when the game was under way but this had made her feel 'anxious and frustrated' because their planning had been inadequate, though not for want of trying.

A player from another group reported he had observed with sympathy the communication problems in this woman's 'programme' and how hard she and her 'commanders' had worked to overcome them. He said that his sympathy was the deciding factor in his determination to release these prisoners when he himself became free.

Peter paraphrased these observations by suggesting the players were saying that however highly individual team-members may be motivated, they need effective support from the group. They agreed with him, which prompted another player to add: 'Goodwill is not enough by itself; somebody's got to know what to do and how to do it!' Peter then left this topic and went on to ask what barriers players had found to communication. Some participants replied that they had become very inhibited when first aware that they were not allowed to speak, nor to use English words, but added that eventually they had worked 'almost intuitively' through body language with their robots to compose a word-list. Peter pursued this line until the discussion turned into a series of statements by players about the importance of trust and openness in communication, the need to work hard at understanding others and the importance of developing good communication skills to achieve these ends.

Then he suggested that the most effective communication skills had been demonstrated by the winning team 'because they won'. He encouraged the members of this team to describe a process of division of labour: how one of them had emerged as a leader and organized the others so that one person was responsible for inventing and miming the command words, another had written them down, another had supervised the robot's memory list, and he himself had directed the robot during play.

Having established to everybody's satisfaction that appropriate division of labour, under a trusted and competent leader, had been a winning strategy, Peter asked the relevant team to comment on their 'planning'. First the winners and then all the participants began to talk as if effective planning had been another key factor in winning the game. The interesting point we noted here was that they might equally well have argued that the successful strategy had not been forward planning at all but, on the contrary, creative improvisation. For example, the winning team had decided to assume they were in a cell with bars like a cage, not a locked room. This eliminated the need to instruct the robot with a command meaning 'unlock the door'. She had only to hand the key to the team leader 'through the bars'. This simplified both her vocabulary and her task, which made her easier to operate than the other robots. Furthermore, it had been the slowest of the three teams that had composed the longest list of words; therefore it could have been said here that planning was an unsuccessful exercise and winning was due instead to imaginative and spontaneous flexibility.

However, Peter gave the group no opportunity to contemplate any possibilities which might have led some players to diverge from the line of thought he wanted them to pursue. For instance, he was quick to point out that the slow team's list was too long for easy reference and suggested that over-planning can be self-defeating, thus leaving intact the message that planning is somehow 'better' than improvisation. Players were the more inclined to agree with this because he had introduced the game from the beginning as a planning exercise and *took this for granted* when he debriefed it.

In this period of time — about three-quarters of an hour — Peter was able to extend players' learning from the game to the real-life activity of directing student theatre. He had no problems in reaching agreement with the group, who plainly felt they had derived new and valuable insights on how to work cooperatively with their drama students. The discussion was animated and enthusiastic and continued for well over an hour.

Of course there is no reason why you should direct and debrief 'Digicon' like this if you do not want to. You may believe the object of games is to give players multiple perspectives on a given issue, rather than to persuade them to reach conclusions predetermined by yourself. According to our argument, it is perfectly possible to use 'Digicon' any way you want, provided you know how to juggle the three golden variables of any game: goal, game and group.

Let us suppose, for example, that you want to play a simulation game as part of a management training course because you want your students to explore experientially and non-judgementally the themes of leadership and power. If you want an 'open' game like this, this is how you might organize and present 'Digicon' — say to a group of managers from various departments within a large organization.

(1) Introduce the game with only the briefest of explanations. The element of the unknown will please some players and alarm or annoy others, which is good. You want to foster differences in people's perception of the game. Keep the scenario as simple as you can.

(2) Organize the players into mixed teams. Do not put people from the same department together. Then set no limit on the invented

command words and allow the prisoners plenty of free discussion in each cell before instructing them to 'programme' their robots. Monitor this process carefully, while appearing to be *laissez-faire*, and note the kinds of disagreements that come up. Identify any emergent leaders and any people who appear unusually passive or aggressive. When debriefing begins after the game, single these people out and direct some questions to them, to give them plenty of opportunity to express mutually divergent views. Remember that while Peter needed a homogeneous group to serve his purpose, yours will best be furthered by encouraging as much heterogeneity in the players as you can. You want multiple perspectives, not consensus.

(3) Make the obstacle course as difficult as reasonably possible and make sure you change over the robots' memory lists before they are 'activated'. You want them to suffer from mixed loyalties between their original team and their new commanders because this ambivalence will be useful in later discussion.

(4) Ignore virtually all cheating, and if you want to permit real aggression, do nothing to prevent the robots' attacking each other physically. Say and do as little as you can while the play is on. The players should feel free to a large extent to restructure the rules. Your objective is that they devote their attention to the process of the game as much as to winning it. The game should be a journey of discovery for them, not a race in which they have eyes only for the finish.

(5) In debriefing, concentrate on what people did, thought, and felt. Elicit as many different kinds of reaction as you can, make it clear that you accept them all as valid, and relate them to themes of leadership and power.

In summary, you need to employ a few alienating devices — including your own 'hands off' behaviour, which some players are likely to resent because they were expecting you to tell them what the game 'meant'. Your intention is to create ambiguity in players' minds rather than 'right answers'.

If you follow this advice we can practically guarantee that there will be a lot of conflict between your players about how they perceived the game — which is what you want. For example, on one occasion when we directed the game the way we have just described, two of three robots complained afterwards of having felt like the mindless puppets of incompetent manipulators who sought power (the key) through the robots' efforts, for which they received no reward. The third robot had worked happily with his commanders and felt satisfied with the relationship. These mutually conflicting responses made for a really useful discussion about the ways in which leadership is perceived by followers.

In debriefing, you give everybody a chance to unload the frustrations and satisfactions they experienced in the game. Then you relate these feelings to the leadership behaviour — the uses of power — that the prisoners employed. You ask open-ended questions that start with the word 'what' rather than 'how'. For example: 'In this situation, what did you do?' instead of: 'This was the problem, how did you solve it?' — because the former question is less judgemental than the latter and is more likely to encourage players to come up with their own, original ideas about leadership.

Now let us look at what you can do with a game like 'New Year's Eve Hat' ('NYEH'), which has a different structure from that of 'Digicon'. It is much more 'open'. As we described in Chapter Six, it requires players to impersonate characters who are handicapped and those who are not. They all have to make paper hats to wear in a fancy hat parade. Some players are physically handicapped by having their thumbs or wrists tied together, by being tied to their chairs, by being blindfolded, and so on.

The game basically is open-ended because it has virtually no rules and permits a wide variety of interpretations. There is no big story build-up, as in 'Digicon', no given crisis to overcome, no pre-set problem to be solved, no shared assumptions about the nature of the task because the criteria for success are arbitrarily decided by the players themselves each time the game is played.

The story and the action begin simultaneously with the players facing a situation rather than a problem. So what do they do? They make hats and wear them in a parade, and judges award prizes to the winners. In theatrical terms, all the action takes place 'on stage'. In 'Digicon' much of the 'action' has already taken place before the game begins. This makes 'NYEH' inherently more existential an experience for the players than 'Digicon' because the characters' existence begins only when the game begins. This gives the role-takers a great deal of freedom. They have no past, only the present, whereas 'Digicon' provides them with a history that they have to 'live up to'.

Theoretically, this makes an 'open' game like 'NYEH' an ideal structure within which to explore alternatives rather than come to conclusions. However, notwithstanding this open framework — which should in principle allow players a great deal of licence — a competent game director can close players' options off to a remarkable extent, and, by changing the form of the game, alter its content.

Our example is the ruthless direction of 'NYEH' by a high school teacher of English literature. Flora wanted her students to derive some clear and unambiguous messages from the game. Flora's class consisted of 23 15-year-old girls and her aim was that they should study the theme of prejudice as it related to a play they were reading — called *The Shifting Heart* — about immigrant settlers and the discrimination they faced. She played 'NYEH' with this class in order to ask them afterwards, 'Were any of the characters in *The Shifting Heart* "handicapped"?' and she wanted an affirmative answer. Throughout the game she adopted a highly authoritarian leadership style, including instructions to the judges about the criteria they should use to assess the hats; and she gave some of the players much more effective materials than the others. This is part of her report to us on the results.

> '. . . They were seated at long trestle tables, ten players, five at each table, facing about seventeen judges . . . and then I began the scenario, and you could have heard a pin drop as I told them this exciting business of the hats. . . And then I went round with string and tied their hands together and tied one hand to a chair. I blindfolded one girl. She was terribly upset about being blind, she really was distressed. . . and another, I tied string right across her two arms, like a thalidomide baby. They were quite horrified by the handicaps . . . I had to say really firmly to the girl with the blindfold: "You are blind!" . . . She had a tiny little scrap of paper to make her hat with, and she said to me, sort of tragically: "Could I have another piece, please?" And I said: "No! Sit down!"'

And the following is part of her report on how the students felt after playing the game:

> 'Immediately people said, "Frustrated", "Annoyed", "Irritated", "Horrible". And I said, "*Good!* Do you think that people who are handicapped all the time might experience those kinds of feelings?" And then we started to talk about the people in *The Shifting Heart* and whether any of them were handi-capped. And that was how I related the game to the play. They were a good class and they came up with: "Yes, they were handicapped because the central family were migrants and this was a handicap for them in the context of the play."'

Flora asked the students to write an essay relating their experiences in 'NYEH' to those of the characters in the play. She awarded the best grade to the essay from which this quotation comes, though she said that all the essays were of a high standard and expressed similar ideas: 'Handicapped people are always discriminated against, whether they have lost an arm, as in the game, or, as in *The Shifting Heart*, they are migrants.

It is hardly surprising that Flora's girls were 'a good class' and 'came up with the right answers'. She used her authority as game leader to impose such harsh constraints on the players during 'NYEH' that she evoked a great deal of frustration and anger. ('It was a screaming match and some of them felt quite cross at the end of it.') She then channelled these emotions into consensus about the suffer-ings of the protagonists in the play-text.

Flora was satisfied that her form of evaluation — the students' essays — gave her the feedback she needed about the learning potential of 'NYEH', which she assessed as high. We think her direction and debriefing of the game, in the context of her teaching aims for that particular group, rank even higher.

Another teacher, Brenda, is our second example of a game leader who directed 'NYEH' and recorded the results for us. We include her account to argue that if you want to achieve your aims for a simulation game, you need to recognize that an essential part of your task will begin when the game ends. This is because, as Peter and Flora demonstrated, debriefing is your final and most powerful method of organizing players' perceptions of the action.

Under Brenda's direction her players created one of the most dramatic versions of 'NYEH' that we have come across. It should have been effective in promoting the kind of learning she wanted her players to acquire, and she thought it had been, but the results of its evaluation by questionnaire were not satisfactory. She was faced with a problem that frequently occurs with gaming as a learning method: the subjective feelings of the game leader appear to be at odds with empirical evidence. We think the answer to this problem lies in the quality of a game's debriefing; Brenda's experience is a case in point.

Brenda, who teaches in a training college for elementary school teachers, played 'NYEH' with a group of 32 students whose average age was 23. She wanted to introduce simulation games to them as a valid, if non-traditional, teaching method. She designed a questionnaire for assessment purposes and adminstered it to the players some time (about a week) after the game, but found that only four out of 32 responses included any reference to gaming as a learning method. The only thing most students felt they had learned was that now they appreciated better the plight of the disabled. Though this conclusion could hardly be criticized, it was disappointing because it was largely irrelevant in the circumstances. Why had the students limited their comments subjectively to the content of the game without also considering it objectively as a form of teaching method? The answer seemed to be that 'NYEH' had provided its young and inexperienced players with a powerful experience, but they were not able to generalize from it to a wider theoretical framework without assistance. Since this had not been given, they had nowhere to locate their feelings except in the game itself.

Brenda directed it so that the players became actors of and audience to a comedy in which clowns derided the antics of victims and fools. She established five players as hat-makers, and handicapped four of them; set up a panel of three judges as caricatures of the public personae of Margaret Thatcher, Nancy Reagan and Princess Diana; and directed the majority of the group (24 people) to be their audience. Thus the form of the game from the beginning was that of popular stage theatre. It is generally accepted that popular theatre is a medium for testing, validating and restating social norms.

The judges performed their parts with such zest that the audience literally shrieked with laughter. 'Mrs Thatcher' introduced the panel by assuming an upper class accent and a manner of great refinement:

> 'May I say what a very great pleasure it is to be invited to judge this competition. As Prime Minister of Great Britain I am delighted to welcome Her Royal Highness the Princess of Wales, and also the distinguished wife of the President of the United States, Mrs Ronald Reagan. Rest assured that our criteria for judging your hats will include not only your personal difficulties but their suitability for this very elite function...'

The panel then proceeded to patronize the handicapped hat-makers and devalue their work, and the audience loved it. At one point 'Mrs Thatcher' said to a severely handicapped contestant: 'Now your hat has a certain impact but we feel that as Princess Diana is here as one of our guests, it is perhaps just a leetle bit pretentious. We can't have a crown-like effect...' (Here her voice on the tape was lost in the gales of laughter from the audience.)

Not surprisingly, some of the handicapped players afterwards expressed feelings of self-pity ('I was upset when she said my hat was tacky; I expected them to say, "Oh, well, she had a hard time making it . . ."'), because the hat-makers had evolved through the role-play into inferior characters and the judges into absurd but powerful figureheads. Therefore it was understandable that these two aspects of the game struck the players most forcibly and were the focus of their questionnaire responses afterwards. Nineteen out of 32 players replied at considerable length that what they had learned from the game was greater awareness of the difficulties faced by the handicapped in real life, not only because of their physical handicaps but also because of the attitudes of some members of society. Seven out of 32 respondents wrote to the effect that though handicapped people are not often openly laughed at in real life (as they were in the game), they may nevertheless be treated as inferior by people who think of themselves, without justification, as being superior.

Thus the players appear to have looked beyond the entertainment value of the game to find a serious meaning in the audience's hilarity and the judges' derision. Nevertheless, their perceptions remained disorganized — though it seems they would have needed only a little help to enable them methodically to contemplate the social value of games as learning strategies. This is what Brenda wanted them to do and they were ready for such reflection after their experience of 'NYEH', but it did not happen.

There are theorists (eg Bergson, 1956) who argue that social laughter is a labelling process, a form of control that serves to identify 'deviant' individuals and thus define, by implication, the way normal people behave. Brenda could have used this line of reasoning to further her objectives. For example she could have suggested that the laughter in the game was partly a socialized response indicating rejection both of the incompetencies of cripples and the pomposity of holders of high office. She could then have gone on to discuss the power of simulation games to explore social processes.

However, she does not seem to have perceived the game as the students did. Her conclusion was that, 'It was enthusiastically received and was a great success — I would run this session again with another group. It was most suitable. They needed to enjoy it themselves to be inspired to try something like it when they are teachers with their own students. The main judge was exceptionally good and provided great entertainment . . .' Thus her focus was on the game's entertainment value as such, rather than its real-world implications. We think this was a pity, because her direction of 'NYEH' was so powerful that it appears to have generated learning potential on a much more profound level than the message that 'games can be fun'. Gaming needs to be taken most seriously when its primary effects seem to be entertaining.

We suggest that this is an example of how the most competent educators can go wrong when they direct simulation games. It also helps to explain why some games seem to work so well for some teachers and not for others. We think game leaders have to organize their goals within a framework of understanding the likely effects of the structure of the game on a particular group of players. The three variables — goal, game and group — must be 'mixed and matched' in effective proportions.

Brenda's inexperience with this total process did not necessarily prevent her, in the long term, from achieving her objective of introducing her students to the advantages of games as a teaching method. She was in regular contact with this group throughout the length of their studies, which extended over several years. It seems likely that the game would have been discussed on a number of occasions and there would be plenty of opportunity for general reflection about simulation games for learning. It is important that game leaders do not feel an overwhelming sense of responsibility to cram as many conclusions as they can into one debriefing. It may be much more effective to titillate players' curiosity to the extent that the game remains in their minds for a long time as an intriguing and stimulating experience to which they will refer again and again when they are reminded of it by real-life events.

Our final case-study of 'NYEH' is of Elaine, a professor in a university school of health administration. She is a founding member of a national gaming association and it was two of her students who were inspired by her to create the original concept from which we derived the game. Therefore, on many counts Elaine is an extremely skilful game leader.

She wanted to use 'NYEH' to argue the case for reverse discrimination, or affirmative action, in employment. That is, she wanted the players to recognize the force of the argument that employment applications from traditionally underprivileged members of the workforce (women, migrants and the handicapped) should receive special consideration. Therefore, like Peter with 'Digicon', her aims were judgemental; but 'NYEH's open structure — without alteration — makes it hard for players to arrive at their game leader's 'right answers'. The action is more likely to induce divergent and inductive thinking than convergent deductions. Elaine, like Peter, interfered with the structure of the game. However, unlike Peter, her manipulations were not altogether successful. We think this is because the composition of her group was more mixed than Peter's and it contained some members who were ideologically opposed to the concepts she wanted to convey via the game.

She introduced 'NYEH' by reminding her players: 'Some of you are going to have to work in personnel departments and you're going to be faced with this issue of discrimination in employment, including the question of whether you give special advantages to people solely on the grounds that they have been discriminated against in the past.' By making this statement Elaine, in effect, gave 'NYEH' a sense of direction that structurally it does not have. As we have said, players' responses to 'NYEH' are likely to be more unpredictable than in a consensual game like 'Digicon', and therefore 'NYEH' is less easy for a game leader to use as a vehicle to advance preselected arguments. You remember that Flora got over the difficulty by giving the judges her own instructions about criteria, eliciting acute emotional responses from the players, and then relating these feelings directly to the study of a play-text. Brenda, on the other hand, engaged her players closely in the process of the game but did not give them enough guidance for them to help her use the game as she originally intended.

Elaine's solution was to inform her students in advance that the game was going to be about discrimination in employment; thus it can be said that she gave the game a background in an attempt to decide its future. Having done this, she went on to describe the game scenario in a fairly authoritarian way, was democratic about handicaps and role allocations, and *laissez-faire* during the play. When debriefing began she made sure the judges' criteria for asessment of the hats were debated, by asking as her first question: 'What comments would you like to make on the judging?'

The first few questions a game leader asks in debriefing are very important because they tend to set the tone for the whole discussion;

leaders may have difficulty in changing it later even if they realize that they began with the 'wrong' questions in terms of their objectives. Peter asked, 'Did you enjoy the game?' and we have already described why we think this was a good opener. Brenda's first question was, 'Why did you laugh so much?', which was perfect for her purpose, but unfortunately she did not use the answer to see it through.

Having started her players on a discussion of the judges' behaviour, Elaine said very little until a player commented: 'I think the judges should have taken into account the disabilities of the hat-makers'. 'Let's talk about that now', said Elaine, and then took a moment to organize the class so that she could command everybody's attention ('If you'll just move around so we can see each other...') before asking the judges to give their reasons for not taking handicaps into account. One of the judges argued that this would have been to judge handicaps, not hats and that 'it would be like giving them a prize for their disability instead of rewarding the best hat. So we decided that judging would be on the best hat and how well it fitted, and originality and use of resources...'

Elaine called for general comments on this, stressing several times that the issue was important and asking again whether women and other underprivileged members of the workforce should receive special treatment to compensate them for past discrimination. She met with some opposition. A player replied that the object of job selection is to advantage the employer, not to disadvantage the employee: 'Because, you know, a female, after working a year or so, may fall pregnant. It's a risk to employ her and in any operation we try to minimize the risk.' Elaine gave this answer short shrift. She said: 'Do you realize that what you're saying is against the present law? You could be taken to court for it.'

She appealed to the judges: 'You two are both women and you made the decision not to compensate the handicapped players for their disability. Do you see the analogy, that in real life you will be professionally discriminated against — you will be "marked down" — because of the disability that you might have a child?' The judges were reluctant at first to accept this argument, but Elaine persisted with it until one woman said, 'I'd want to be assessed the same as a male applicant. I'd want to be equal.'

One player was firm in his refusal to accept the concept of affirmative action. He persisted in his argument that women are poorer employment risks than men and to compensate them for being so would be to invite economic disaster. Finally Elaine told him: 'I can guarantee that your attitude will have no effect on the assessment that I shall make of your studies in this course, but it will have an effect on your future, and it's important for you to realize that.

What you should be thinking about is how to make your organization flexible enough to take account of women's lifestyles, because you're going to be stuck with them whether you like it or not.'

Thus Elaine worked hard to present her viewpoint via 'NYEH', including what might seem to be unscrupulous behaviour on her part, since it consisted of a veiled reminder to one student that she had the power to 'fail' him if he disagreed with her. Nevertheless, given that game, that goal, and that particular group, we do not know any game leader who could have done better. The participants were mostly very conservative and held traditional views about the employment of women. Affirmative action was a new concept to them and they had difficulty with it. As it was, Elaine's introduction to and debriefing of 'NYEH' succeeded in changing the attitudes of at least some of them from outright rejection to thoughtfulness and even a degree of acceptance. She might have done better if she had interfered more with the game itself, as Flora did, by giving the judges the criteria they should use. Or perhaps she could have cast some of the handicapped characters as women, and given them an egg to hold while they made their hats. This could have simulated the problems that working mothers have with pregnancy and childcare. A game leader may have to work hard to subvert some game structures.

Our final case-study is of a beautifully relaxed debriefing of 'Gerontology' in which the shape of the game, the game leader's objectives, and the temperament of the group came together in a most harmonious way.

'Gerontology' is the most open of all the games we have described in previous chapters. The participants sit on chairs, which represent their homes. They are tied to the chairs with ropes, which represent their mobility. They are given paperclips to represent money and a paper and pencil as their 'memory'. They are told that they are in the role of old people in society and that there is a 'bank' and a 'welfare agency' to which they can go if they need help. Periodically the 'Grim Reaper' plagues them with illness, poverty, or death. Apart from these constraints, they can do whatever they please and create whatever kind of community they want.

A friend of ours, Erica, played 'Gerontology' with a group of health professionals: doctors, senior nurses and adminstrators from Asia and the Pacific. When the game was over she introduced the debriefing as follows:

'All of you are going to be working as health professionals with old people. What is there in this game that you can learn about dealing with the aged in our society? Given a society that says you shouldn't let people commit suicide, or that you shouldn't kill them off, do you think we ought to do anything different about old age, as people and as administrators?'

Note that she said this *after* the game, not before it. Thus she did not interfere with its structure.

She pointed out that there had been a marked difference in role behaviour between two people, Sandra and Alastair, who had played the parts of welfare officers. The other participants agreed with her. One player complained that Sandra had been so authoritarian that 'I couldn't be bothered hassling with her', while another praised the 'compassion' of Alastair, who was generous with public funds. Erica asked: 'Does that mean that people can't be bothered dealing with bureaucrats if there are alternatives available in society? Is that one of the reasons the compassionate agencies are always out of money?' This was a question to provoke inductive thinking in the players. That is, Erica picked up one person's individual observation about something that had happened in the game and made it the basis for a general question about the real-life analogy.

She was also quick to enlarge on other points that she wanted the players to discuss. For example, when a man said that in the game he had refused to help 'poor Alan' because he was suffering from a 'terminal disease' and was 'too far gone', Erica asked, 'Does that mean there's no point in us trying to help someone who has no hope?' This prompted an Asian player to comment: 'I found the meaning of life when I got hospitalized. It wasn't the security that really mattered. I realized that I wanted to live. I was struggling all the time to live.' His statement stimulated a discussion about the quality of life for old people in different cultures. An American participant said he thought that in middle-class white American culture, 'a lot of old people are quite glad to be rid of the burden' (ie to die). Someone else challenged him on this by saying: 'Just because we think old people have no purpose doesn't mean they think like that'. Another player added: 'I was feeling like that [when I was in role as an old person]. I didn't have any friends and I was ready to die. But the next minute, friends came to my aid and I suddenly felt rejuvenated and exhilarated.' The discussion proceeded along these lines until some group members spontaneously began to suggest some possible real-life alternatives for old people, such as: 'What's wrong with people over 65 forming their own cooperatives?'

Thus the discussion focused throughout on what had happened in the game rather than on how players had solved a predetermined problem — which gave Erica a great deal of freedom to range outwards from the game experiences to encourage a kind of brainstorm for creative thinking about old people's place in society, the contributions they can make, and the special needs they may have.

The above are only a few examples of our research findings, which led us to create the following table. It summarizes what we have suggested so far about how you can organize a game, including its debriefing, so that its content conveys to players the meanings that you intend.

Closed Games	Open Games
'This is the problem: how will we solve it?'	'This is the situation: what will you do?'
(1) Players are encouraged by leader's preliminary remarks or warm-up to make the same general assumptions about the game and to create a feeling of 'togetherness'.	Preliminary discussion or warm-up is aimed to reveal heterogeneity of group and disparity between members' views. views.
(2) The leader is perceived as a benevolent authority figure.	Players are not encouraged to look to the director for a lead (which may cause feelings of resentment).
(3) Differences between players are shown to be functional by encouraging division of labour.	Differences between players are not assumed to be functional. Therefore conflict is more likely to arise.
(4) Leader forms teams, gives instructions, sets the scene, answers questions; is seen to be in control.	Leader says and does as little as possible.
(5) The setting of the game and the characters have a 'past'. Players are asked to imagine events that happened prior to the action of the game. They begin at a point of crisis.	The game setting has no 'past' and all the action takes place 'on stage'. Players are offered a situation, not presented with a crisis.
(6) The characters are constrained by detailed information and specific role instructions.	There are few rules, little detail is provided, therefore there is opportunity for chance happenings on the whims of the players.
(7) Players are organized into teams or sub-groups. They all play by the same rules.	Number and arrangement of players are comparatively unimportant. Groups may have uneven numbers, or individuals may work alone. Some interpret the rules differently from others.
(8) The players' point of attack is a moment of crisis.	The players embark on a journey rather than grapple with a crisis. Thus there are multiple plots and diffuse action.
(9) There are distinct steps or stages in the game, directed by the leader and occurring at fairly regular intervals with the aim and effect of progressing the action along specific lines. There is a sense of order and regular pace.	Stages in the game are not clearly marked. Some seem more important than others. Changes occur because of the activities of the players and are due to general causes. Pace and rhythm vary. There is no sense or order and balance.

Closed Games	*Open Games*
(10) Each step proceeds logically from the one before. The action is goal-oriented and forward looking.	Minor actions spin off from major ones in an apparently illogical manner. The characters are process-minded and present-oriented.
(11) There is a single line of mounting pressure, with stimulus towards cooperative problem-solving and emphasis on outcome.	Emphasis is on players' reactions to the situation as it develops; less compression of events, more chance happenings. Events are diverse, emphasis is on behaviour, not outcome.
(12) Players' choices become increasingly limited as events close in to constrain them.	There are multiple lines of action, a need for individual decisions. Events do not accumulate to confine the players.
(13) Observers' interest focuses on how the players will solve the problem rather than what they are doing, which tends to predetermine the nature of the outcomes; there is a sense of inevitability.	Players act autonomously, constrained only by their real-life restraints. There is room for 'deviant' (minority) opinion and behaviour.
(14) Players derive pleasure from shared experience. Conflict is seen as reconciliatory. There are problems and answers.	Players find themselves more thoughtful than pleased. There is a lack of certainty and an awareness of new possibilities.

We finish this chapter with a brief discussion of evaluation methods for simulation games. One of the problems with most standard techniques such as feedback questionnaires is that they are not really designed for games. They are intended for students to assess more traditional teaching methods such as lectures or demonstrations. Therefore they contain questions like: 'How do you rate the lecturer's presentation on a scale of one to five?' However, when a game is the learning strategy it often happens that the participants retain either an exaggerated respect or a residual anger for a game leader who has provided them with a powerful experience which has stimulated them greatly, or with which they may not have been entirely comfortable. These heightened feelings usually gain their proper perspective with time and are a natural part of the change process we call learning. But while they last they can play havoc with empirical assessment if it is made too soon after the game event. On the other hand, as indicated by Brenda's use of open-ended questionnaires, such feedback can be extremely useful in spotting weaknesses in the game leader's presentation.

Another problem in evaluating games is that games are often

played as part of a course, seminar, or workshop and it is difficult to sort out which learning came from what method because there is overlap. If the game is played at the beginning of a seminar and then assessed, this is likely to penalize the game or to give it undeserved credit, depending on players' reactions.

We have already mentioned two evaluation methods that game leaders use — essay and open-ended questionnaire. Each was considered effective by Flora and Brenda, respectively, though we consider that Brenda could have learned more from her students' replies than perhaps she did. Another comment is that essay writing by players after a game has the advantage that it effectively reinforces any learning the game may have induced by being itself another kind of learning method. It is true that open-ended questionnaires can become mini-essays if the respondents feel strongly about their replies, as Brenda's students did. However, in our experience, such lengthy replies are an exception rather than the rule. Most respondents reply very briefly to questionnaires, which is not usually satisfactory where games are concerned because more detailed feedback is required.

We like to use a game to assess games. We call it 'Contract' and we reckon it is as good a way as any, and better than some, to get honest feedback from the players about what they think they have learned. It is designed to evaluate the learning from games (or a single game) that are part of a course in which other teaching methods have been used, but it can be adapted fairly easily if you want to use the concept to evaluate a game as a single experience on its own. It works on the same principle as all 'closed' games — its structure persuades the group towards consensus. But to guard against partiality on the part of the game leader, it is better to ask a colleague — or one of the players — to act as leader in place of yourself. You should be present — because you will learn a lot — but only as a non-participant observer.

'Contract'

(1) The director forms people into several groups, each consisting of three to seven people.
(2) Each group is asked to elect a representative who will summarize the feelings of the group after discussing the questions below.
(3) The groups privately discuss their replies to these questions (they may prefer to go to another room):
  (a) What did you not like about the game (including the game director)?
  (b) What did you like about it?

    (c) What did you find least helpful personally?

    (d) What did you find helpful?

    (e) What are your goals for this course/seminar/workshop/ whatever? More theory? New behaviour? New contracts? Peer interaction? What else?

    (f) What learning methods do you think will help you most? Lectures? Discussions? Reading? More games? What else?

    (g) What do you have to contribute to the group's learning? What are your special skills, aptitudes and experience?

(4) When the teams have discussed the above (about 15 minutes or longer if they wish) they all meet in plenary session and each team representative is 'interviewed' by the director, who repeats the above questions out loud in front of everybody. In reply each representative in turn summarizes the feelings of his or her team members on each question and the director posts the replies.

(5) The director now throws the game open to general discussion. Any group member can ask anybody any question.

(6) The director summarizes the whole exercise by drawing up a verbal contract to exist from now on between the original game leader and the participants, each agreeing to contribute to the aims of the group as a whole, in the ways that have been previously discussed. If the game leader will take no more part in the rest of the course or seminar (because other presenters will be in charge of the remaining material), the contract will be in two parts. One part will be in the form of an undertaking by the leader to bear in mind the directives of the group and act on them when playing games in the future. The other part will be an undertaking by the group to apply what they have learned about themselves to the rest of the course.

This description of 'Contract' should make it clear why the leader of the game that has been evaluated should not be the director of this feedback exercise. It is the director's business often to summarize the summaries of each team leader, in order to post succinct responses on the board or flipchart and then to use this information to create the 'contract'. We have already made it clear that a game leader's behaviour is one of the three critical components of all games; and it is all too easy, as we know from having done it, for a game leader to manipulate 'Contract' — without either the leader or the participants being consciously aware of it — so that its results are more favourable to a game's evaluation than they might otherwise appear. Hence the need for an impartial director.

/

Epilogue

This book has discussed a learning method which we have called 'gaming'. We have used it to mean a directed group activity that is often called by other names, like simulation games, structured experiences, structured role-plays, even 'behaviour rehearsals'. Some teachers seem to assume that all of these are different — for example, some people distinguish between them in terms of rules, incentives and goals; thus a 'structured role-play' is described by Livingston and Stoll (1973) as having fewer rules, less structure, and different goals than a 'simulation game'. We argue that they are all essentially the same. A great many books of simulation games and structured experiences are available, full of detailed information and practical advice about how to direct such activities in the classroom. Thousands of teachers all over the world use them regularly as a learning strategy and are very satisfied with the results.

The only problem we have found with all this literature is that no amount of practical advice can cover all eventualities unless such advice includes a theoretical component. For example, people who are interested in computers can learn a great deal about how to operate them from a relevant manual; but unless they also understand how computers 'work' they will continue on a trial and error basis to tinker with bits and pieces of the technology without recognizing them as parts of a functioning system. Likewise, the tendency of many game directors, in our observation, is to fall back on practical experience and to experiment when a game does not go according to their expectations (some theorists, such as Elgood (1981) for example, specifically recommend this *ad hoc* approach). Such leaders use their personalities and professional expertise to induce momentum in apparently reluctant learners and thus 'get the game going' — which is why they tend to describe gaming as a fail-safe learning method because 'something always happens'.

We have concluded that there are three major disadvantages to these survival strategies by game leaders:

(1) The survivors learn little from their experiences — except perhaps increased self-confidence — because they have not analysed theoretically what went wrong, what went right, and why.

(2) If game leaders take an improvisational attitude towards games, this may discourage newcomers. For example, many teachers prefer to plan and organize their material cumulatively. If they perceive the outcomes of gaming to be speculative, they will tend to avoid using it. They are thus denied the opportunity to discover how rich games are in learning potential.

(3) Many people who are asked to take part in a learning game in a spirit of 'everybody must play' and 'let's see what happens' are not temperamentally suited to this approach. Some learners seem intuitively to dislike a learning method that stresses action and experience at the expense of observation and theory.

We accept that gaming is a strategy that depends for success on three apparently chance variables:

(1) The personality of the game leader;
(2) The temperament of the players as a group;
(3) The game itself, including the ways in which it is organized and presented to the players.

What we have tried to do in this book is to demonstrate some of the most likely ways that these variables will operate in combination, and why. We have described how we think leaders can control a game to be a teaching method whose results are reasonably predictable — as much as those of any more traditional method. Therefore, there is a kind of double message in our title, *Leadership Training Through Gaming*. It is intended to mean not only that you can impart some leadership skills to your learners through playing games with them, but also that you yourself are likely to learn a great deal about leadership in the process. We have argued that the form of a game will influence its content. We hope the same is true of this book.

Appendix: Alphabetical Summary of Games

Note: It is assumed for all the following games that writing materials will be available for the players, as well as all the usual articles and furnishings that one can expect in the average seminar room such as tables or desks, chairs, etc.

'A to B'

Objectives: To reveal individual differences in group members' perceptions of a problem and therefore the differences in their proposed solutions.
Duration: About half an hour.
Number of players: Any number.
Materials: None.
Summary: Puzzle whose solution requires abstract, logical thinking.

'Auction'

Objectives:
(1) To study the behaviour of emergent leaders.
(2) To study follower motivation and behaviour.
Duration: Two hours.
Number of players: About seven to any number.
Materials:
(1) One copy of the rules for each player, as described in the game;
(2) A money 'float', the amount to depend on the number of players.
Summary: Players as individuals bid for a cash pot, over an indefinite number of rounds. They find that they must cooperate or they will lose their money, but must beat the others to win.

'Behave Yourself'

Objectives: To demonstrate that:
(1) Human behaviour is a constant phenomenon.

(2) People cannot 'not behave'.
(3) We signal messages to each other all the time, whether we know it or not.
(4) Leaders need to be aware of the impressions their behaviour makes on their followers.

Duration: About half an hour.
Number of players: At least four.
Materials: Role cards as described in the game.
Summary: In pairs, players assume the role behaviour described on their instruction cards and then discuss the experience.

'Brainstorm'

Objectives:
(1) To generate a lot of ideas quickly.
(2) To promote creative thinking.
(3) For cross-cultural groups: to integrate and develop language skills.

Duration: About an hour.
Number of players: About seven people to any number.
Materials: Butchers' paper and felt-tipped pens.
Summary: Groups of about seven people are formed, each with a volunteer who specifies a subject or problem about which he or she would like to be brainstormed. Reporters record the brainstorms and the players then discuss the outcomes in plenary session.

'Broken Squares'

Objectives:
(1) To study group behaviour.
(2) To promote group dynamics.

Duration: About half an hour.
Number of players: Minimum of five, to any number.
Materials: A set of squares for each team of five players, as illustrated in Figure 1: Broken Squares. A set consists of five envelopes with pieces of cardboard cut into different patterns. When all the pieces are arranged, from all the envelopes, the players will find they have between them five squares of equal size.

To prepare a set, cut out five cardboard squares, each side exactly 6 inches long. Place the squares in a row and mark them as in Figure 1, pencilling the letters lightly so they can be erased. Then cut them out. Label the envelopes from 1 to 5 and fill them with the puzzle pieces as follows:

Envelope	Pieces
1	I, H, E
2	A, A, A, C
3	A, J
4	D, F
5	G, B, F, C

Erase the pencilled letter from each piece as you put it into its envelope and mark it instead with the number of the appropriate envelope. This makes it easy to sort the pieces out again after the game.

Summary: In groups of five, players have to build squares out of the puzzle pieces.

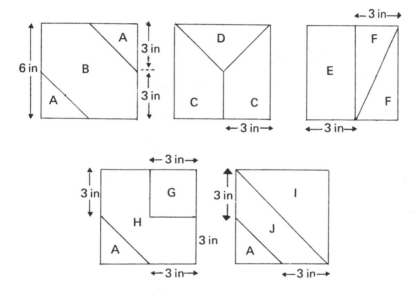

Figure 1: *'Broken Squares'*

'Digicon'

Objectives:
(1) To study leader-follower behaviour.
(2) To provide a planning exercise.
Duration: About an hour.
Number of players: At least eight.
Materials: None.
Summary: The players are in role as prisoners and robots. The robots have to be instructed by the prisoners on how to free them. The robots have a limited memory bank and will respond to individual commands. The prisoners have to plan the commands that they will need to operate the robots effectively.

'Down it Goes'

Objectives:
(1) For biology or natural science classes, or for teacher training: to illustrate the process of digestion in the human body.
(2) To provide opportunity for young players to work as a team towards a common task.
Duration: At least an hour.
Number of players: Minimum of about 15.
Materials: Blackboard or flipchart to display diagram of body machine.
Summary: The players assume the roles of parts in the digestive system, eg jaws, gut, enzymes, etc, and form a human body machine to simulate the process of digestion.

'The Egg Adoption Project'

Objective: To give young people insights into parent-child relationships.
Duration: One week.
Number of players: Any number.
Materials:
(1) One raw egg in its shell for each player.
(2) A notebook for each player, in which to keep a diary of the week's events concerning the egg.
Summary: Players are required to 'parent' an egg for a week and report on the experience.

'Either...Or'

Objectives: To increase participants' self-knowledge and group members' awareness of each other's differences.
Duration: About three-quarters of an hour.
Number of players: Any number.
Summary: Players form a line down the middle of the room. Director asks a series of questions requiring either-or answers and players move to the left or the right according to their replies; then they explain their choices.

'Fit or Fat?'

Objectives:
(1) For school students: to demonstrate that people use foods in different ways, depending on their body's needs.

(2) To encourage good general eating and keep-fit habits.
Duration: About an hour.
Number of players: At least about eight.
Materials:
(1) A chair for each player.
(2) A pair of dice in a cup.
(3) A packet of balloons.
(4) A skipping rope.
(5) A glass of water.
(6) A stand-on weighing scale.
(7) A set of written forfeit cards, as described in the game.
Summary: Players advance round a circle of chairs according to their throwing of the dice. Other players are seated at intervals on the chairs to represent 'snakes' (as in the game of Snakes and Ladders). They hold the forfeit cards. If a player 'lands' on a 'snake' he or she has to draw and perform a forfeit.

'The Five-Pound Note'

Objective: To provide practice in negotiation.
Duration: About 20 minutes.
Number of players: Any number over three.
Materials: A five-pound note (or similar currency).
Summary: Players bid for a five-pound note. All bids are forfeit to the auctioneer.

'Gene Scene'

Objectives:
(1) To demonstrate the chance factor in genetic inheritance.
(2) To suggest the twin notions of dominant and recessive genes and some possible results of their combinations.
(3) To indicate some degree of inevitability in the inheritance of certain individual physical characteristics.
(4) To illustrate the discreteness of some genetic characteristics.
(5) To promote facility in working out some possible genetic combinations, which includes practice in elementary mathematical skills.
Duration: About two hours.
Number of players: From about eight to 20.
Materials: The following charts will be needed for display.

The eye colour brown is from a dominant gene; the eye colour blue is from a recessive gene. You have inherited 50 per cent of your genes (half of them) from your mother and 50 per cent from your father.

If you have blue eyes, this is because your inherited genes for eye colour are blue. Therefore write bb on your label (b = blue).

If you have brown eyes, at least one of your inherited genes for eye colour must be brown. Your symbol therefore will be either BB (B = brown) or bB. You do not know which it is, but for the purpose of the game you can choose to write either.

When you have written either bb or BB or bB on your label in large letters, stick it on to your forehead so everybody can see it.

Figure 1: *Gene Chart*

This diagram shows what might happen when six couples, with various combinations of eye colour between them, each have four children:

— bb and bb will produce: bb, bb, bb and bb (all children will have blue eyes)

— bb and bB will produce: bb, bB, bb and Bb (any of their children will have a 50 per cent chance of blue or brown eyes)

— bb and BB will produce: bB, Bb, Bb, and Bb (all children will have brown eyes)

— BB and BB will produce: BB, BB, BB and BB (all children will have brown eyes)

— bB and BB will produce: bB, bB, BB and BB (all children will have brown eyes)

— bB and bB will produce: bb, bB, bB and BB (any child has a 25 per cent chance of blue eyes and a 75 per cent chance of brown eyes)

If A is blue-eyed and Z is brown-eyed the following are possible combinations of eye-colour for their children:

There will be a 25 per cent chance of any child having blue eyes and a 75 per cent chance of any child having brown eyes: that is:

bb + bB (or BB) will produce: bb, bB, bb, bB, bb, bB, bB, bB, bB, bB, bB, bB.

Figure 2: *Blue eyes = bb. Brown eyes = BB or bB.*

'Gerontology'

Objectives:

(1) To provide the players with experiences analogous to those of being poor and old in the community.

(2) To have the responsibility of providing services for the old and infirm.

Duration: At least two hours.
Number of players: At least 12 to 18 and preferably more.
Materials:
(1) Short lengths of rope, about three times as many as there are players (each rope should be about 18 inches long).
(2) At least one large packet of paperclips..
(3) Grim Reaper cards, as described in the game.
Summary: Most of the players are in role as old people. Their chairs represent their residences to which they are tied by lengths of rope to represent their mobility. Paperclips represent their worldly wealth. A few players are in role as bank managers and welfare service representatives. The players have to create their own society under the shadow of the Grim Reaper, who visits them periodically with disablement or death.

'Grapevine'

Objective: To study some basic concepts of communication systems in organizational settings (for school students as well as older people).
Duration: About an hour.
Number of players: At least 12 players.
Materials:
(1) Stopwatch.
(2) Pack of playing cards.
(3) Pencils and a stack of paper for the players.
(4) Adhesive labels.
Summary: Competitive teams simulate two kinds of group communication process, then compare and contrast them.

'Harry's Dog'

Objective: To study people's problem-solving behaviour.
Duration: About half an hour.
Number of players: Any number over three.
Summary: A problem-solving exercise.

'Identikit'

Objective: To study possible connections between leadership effectiveness and the personal presentation of the leader.
Duration: About an hour.
Number of players: From three to 25.
Summary: Players assemble symbolic portraits of famous leaders, from a collage of photographs, and then discuss their selections.

'Infernal Towers'

Objective: To show some of the blocks in communication that come from people's tendency to assume that their 'reality' is the same as that of everybody else.
Duration: About an hour.
Number of players: At least six.
Materials:
(1) A large quantity of Lego or similar building bricks.
(2) Instruction cards for each player, as described in the game.
Summary: In teams of six people each, the players have to build a tower. They have all been given private instructions, some of which are in mutual conflict. The players have to negotiate in silence.

'Making Money'

Objective: To study leadership power in small groups.
Duration: About two hours.
Number of players: Any number over five.
Materials: A large amount of small change, or Smarties (M & M's) if the players do not want to play with real money.
Summary: In sub-groups of three to seven people, each player begins with the same stake. At the end of a ten-minute round the player in each group who has increased the stake by the highest amount becomes the leader of the group in the next round and sets the rules of play.

'Model Aeroplanes'

Objectives: In a cost-productivity exercise
(1) To study team behaviour.
(2) To study leadership behaviour.
Duration: At least two hours.
Number of players: At least ten.
Materials:
(1) Lots of sheets of paper.
(2) A template for the aeroplane design, if this is required.
Summary: In teams, the players have to buy paper, make model aeroplanes and sell them to designated buyers who put them through a quality control test before purchase. The team with the biggest profit wins the game.

'Money in the Middle'

Objective: To study decision-making behaviour in groups.
Duration: About half an hour.
Number of players: Any number over five.
Materials: A small cash sum for each player.
Summary: All the players' money is placed in the middle of a circle of people and the whole sum awarded to one player on the consensus decision of the group.

'My Car Won't Start'

Objectives:
(1) To study different problem-solving styles.
(2) To serve as an illustration of the uses of games that require nothing but the imagination of the players.
Duration: About half an hour.
Number of players: Any number over three.
Summary: An exercise in problem-solving.

'New Year's Eve Hat'

Objective: To study the social experience of physical handicaps.
Duration: About two hours.
Number of players: At least eight.
Materials:
(1) Sheets of coloured crepe paper.
(2) Scissors.
(3) Cellophane tape.
(4) A stapler and/or pins.
(5) Balloons, ribbons and other decorations.
(6) Soft materials to handicap the players.
Summary: Some of the players have to make hats to wear in a party parade; others take the role of judges. Most of the hat-makers are physically handicapped by having one hand tied behind their back, or to a chair, or by being blindfolded, and so on.

'The Photocopy Machine'

Objective: To study leaders' negotiation skills.
Duration: One half to one hour.
Number of players: At least four.

Materials: None.
Summary: Players take it in turn to perform a role-play between two people. A manager seeks to persuade a reluctant employee to work late to finish an urgent assignment.

'Picnic'

Objectives:
(1) To encourage creative problem-solving in young people.
(2) To demonstrate the advantages of planning skills.
(3) To develop concentration.
(4) To increase motivation in groups of young learners.
(5) To promote self-leadership in young people.
Duration: At least an hour, and can be extended over several sessions.
Number of players: From eight upwards.
Materials: None.
Summary: The group has to plan an activity and carry it out; then discuss what happened.

'Ponsonby'

Objectives:
(1) To demonstrate how assumptions about the nature of a task can affect the behaviour of the group.
(2) To demonstrate to game leaders that game materials can be found in the most unlikely places.
Duration: Two hours.
Number of players: At least 20.
Summary: Carpet squares are used to create a competitive team game in which one team has received different instructions from the other about the nature of the game.

'The Princess and the Peasant'

Objective: To study the differences in the ways people solve problems.
Duration: About 20 minutes.
Number of players: Any number over three.
Materials: None.
Summary: A problem-solving exercise.

'Quote Me a Price'

Objective: To experience an exercise in negotiation skills.
Duration: About 20 minutes.
Number of players: Minimum of two.
Materials: An object over which a seller and a buyer can haggle.
Summary: One player attempts to sell an object to another. Then the group discusses their negotiation strategies.

'The Road Game'

Objectives:
(1) To study leadership power.
(2) To study economic imperatives, pressures of public opinion, and players' priorities concerning the quality of their lives.
Duration: At least two hours.
Number of players: About 20 to 35 people, though the game can be played with as few as 12.
Materials:
(1) Four sheets of thin drawing cardboard in different colours.
(2) Masking tape.
(3) Four coloured felt-tipped pens.
Summary: A drawing board made of the four pieces of cardboard represents a 'map' of four different countries. Players form four groups to represent the respective citizens of each country. The object of the game is to draw roads within and between each country. Some roads receive a money subsidy from the bank. The leaders of each country negotiate with each other about the positioning of the roads.

'Roger's Game'

Objectives:
(1) To illustrate how leaders can create assumptions about the nature of a task so followers will support their leader's actions.
(2) To discuss the meanings of 'winning' and 'losing'.
Duration: About half an hour.
Number of players: From about eight to 25.
Materials:
(1) A blackboard or whiteboard on which to post the diagram.
(2) Coloured chalks or pens for the players.
Summary: The game is announced to be about winning and losing. Players each contribute a small sum to the pot. Director posts a

matrix of 36 (6 × 6) squares, and selects two team leaders, who pick their teams. Team-members take turns to make zeros or crosses on the board squares, each team to complete as many lines as possible, each line to win a proportion of the pot. The results are discussed in terms of the assumptions and behaviour of the game leader, the team leaders, and the followers.

'Ships of the Line'

Objective: To study people's problem-solving behaviour.
Duration: About half an hour.
Number of players: Any number over three.
Summary: A problem-solving exercise.

'The Shoe Saleswoman'

Objective: To study people's problem-solving behaviour.
Duration: About half an hour.
Number of players: Any number over three.
Summary: A problem-solving exercise.

'Simultaneous Interpretation'

Objectives:
(1) To improve individuals' concentration.
(2) To promote empathy between group members.
Duration: About 20 minutes.
Number of players: Any number.
Summary: In a large circle, group members in turn repeat the words of the first speaker, until they get back to the speaker as an 'echo'.

'Smarties'

Objective: To provide a simulation of an organizational experience where workers' welfare is at odds with management's views on high productivity.
Duration: About two hours.
Number of players: At least ten.
Materials:
(1) A very large quantity of chocolate pieces (Smarties or M&M's).
(2) A 'float' of small change.

(3) A large container of water or soft drink.

(4) A large supply of plastic cups.

Summary: Players take the roles of managers, workers, union representatives, consumers, health professionals and conservationists. The managers pay the workers according to the amount of Smarties they consume or persuade others to consume. The other characters try to modify or prevent this on health grounds.

'Status'

Objective: To examine the views of the group on the connections between individuals' occupations and their social status.

Duration: About half an hour.

Number of players: Any number over seven.

Materials: Adhesive labels, one for each player.

Summary: Players are labelled with different occupations and asked to rank themselves according to their perceived status, in a line down the middle of the room; then to discuss the final line-up.

'Talking Heads'

Objective: To study cross-cultural negotiation.

Duration: One day.

Number of players: At least eight.

Materials: Instructions for each participant as below and as described in the game.

Summary: The participants have two tasks:

(1) To make recommendations concerning proposed changes for an imaginary company called Saito Corporation.

(2) To recommend a single corporate language for Saito Corporation's international communication. They are required to adopt certain positions, which are outlined on cue cards they receive at the beginning of the game. These may or may not be opinions that correspond to their own views, but nevertheless it will be their task to argue in support of them as effectively as they can.

All players are given the same general scenario, which is as follows:

In 1950 Saito Corporation, a petrochemical company, had an export department which took care of its foreign business. The company had only two small overseas branches and foreign sales accounted for about 7 per cent of its total business.

The manager in charge of the export department was supervised by the vice president for marketing as shown in Figure 1. The language

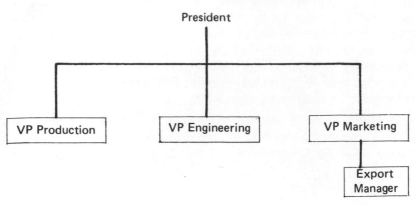

Figure 1 : Saito Corporation 1950

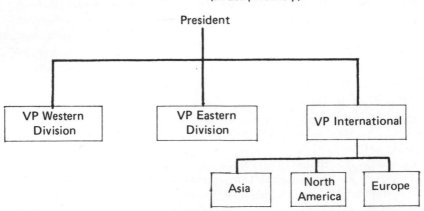

Figure 2: Saito Corporation 1965
(in use presently)

was, of course, Japanese. This organizational structure worked well until the 1960s when Saito began to make major foreign investments. In 1965 the company was restructured as shown in Figure 2.

The 1965 reorganizational structure, which remains today, was done according to geographical region, with vice presidents for major Japanese areas as well as an international vice president. Presently all country managers outside Japan report to and are supervised by this international vice president. Each country is managed largely by local staff, using the local language. In a few cases the manager is a Japanese national. Company reports and all international mail are written in the local language with a translation in Japanese.

A few years ago major problems began developing within the international section. The expansion of markets led to the creation of more divisions, and these divisions have become more and more involved with one another. The US division now communicates frequently with the West German division, while the Taiwan division is frequently in contact with the French and Italian divisions. There is a lack of coordination, however, and confusion is common as the divisions try to work with each other.

As shown in Figure 2, in 1965 there were only three foreign divisions but now there are 13 with sales amounting to 50 per cent of the total business of Saito Corporation. Of this 50 per cent, 25 per cent is in Asia, 14 per cent in Europe, and 11 per cent in the Americas, ie, 8 per cent in the US and 3 per cent in Brazil. The president and Board of Directors are now considering a proposal for an organizational restructuring as shown in Figure 3.

Under this new plan it is suggested that there be five vice presidents: one each for North America, South America, Europe, Asia, and Japan. All of the individual national divisions are to be directed by managers who will report directly to their respective vice president. The goal of the reorganization is to coordinate production and marketing efforts across the entire corporation. Many company leaders believe that a single language must be chosen as the international language of Saito if that goal is to be achieved.

As a country manager, you have been invited to meet with other managers in order to choose an international language for Saito and to review the proposed organizational changes for the company (Figure 3). The recommendations made by this group will be sent to the President and Board of Directors and are likely to be followed.

The players also receive a copy each of the three figures referred to, and a copy of the 'conference agenda'. The role-players each get a copy of their individual role instructions.

'Talking Heads': Conference Agenda

(1) Welcome delegates; explain tasks of the conference.
(2) Self-introduction of delegates.
(3) Divide group into three committees:
     Committee 1: Ramifications of proposed changes in Saito Corporation;
     Committee 2: The uses for a single international language;
     Committee 3: The criteria for the selection of the international language.
(4) Committees' reports to the entire group.

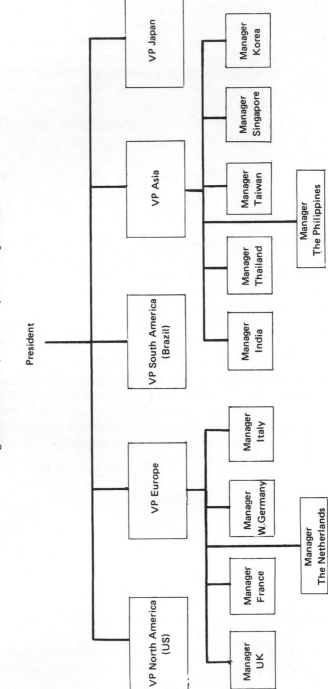

Figure 3: Saito Corporation Proposed Reorganization

(5) Recommendations for the acceptance of the proposed changes in Saito Corporation.
(6) Open discussion.
(7) Voting (voting continues until one plan receives two-thirds of the votes cast).
(8) Call for nomination of international language for Saito Corporation.
(9) Open discussion.
(10) Voting to select language (voting continues until one language receives two-thirds of the votes).

Participant Cue Card for Manager from Korea

You are a member of a conference which is to make recommendations to the Head Office (the President and Board of Directors) in Tokyo on the proposed changes in the corporate structure, and in the selection of an international language.

Your particular concern is to ensure that the following are adequately incorporated into the suggestions for the corporation:

(1) *Dealing with the proposed reorganization:*
The plans for reorganization seem to be simple and to involve few major changes. It seems to you that these plans merely reflect the present corporate structure and that is good.
(2) *Dealing with the selection of an international language:*
You like very much the idea of having a single international language. You believe it is time for Saito (at least internationally) to drop its attachment to Japanese. If a single language is chosen, it will help your situation in Korea a great deal. Koreans are still unhappy about the Japanese occupation of Korea and they do not like to speak Japanese although many are still able to do so. If Saito is going to grow in Korea, a single language policy is necessary. You believe English would be the best choice.

In order to make certain that your points are properly dealt with by fellow delegates of the conference, it may be necessary to bring them up several times during the discussions. Be prepared to make and suggest compromises if necessary.

Participant Cue Card for Manager from Thailand, who is a Japanese National, since no Local Thai Manager has yet been Found

You are a member of a conference which is to make recommendations to the Head Office (the President and Board of Directors) in Tokyo on the proposed changes in the corporate structure, and in the selection of an international language.

Your particular concern is to ensure that the following are adequately incorporated into the suggestions for the corporation:

(1) *Dealing with the proposed reorganization:*
This reorganization does not deal at all with the problems you are having in Thailand. The Thai attitude towards work is very different from that of the Japanese, and although you have learned to speak a little Thai, you still have real trouble in supervising Thais. They do not seem to know how to take the hints you give and when you speak directly to them in any negative way, they become insulted. In the three years you have been there you have had eight translators quit the job. The ninth one presently seems to be under a great deal of stress. You would like this conference to deal with this reorganization plan quickly and then discuss the more important matters of managing cultural differences.

(2) *Dealing with the selection of an international language:*
Your choice is Japanese or English, maybe both, but no other single language or combination of languages is possible for you.

In order to make certain that your points are properly dealt with by fellow delegates of the conference, it may be necessary to bring them up several times during the discussions. Be prepared to make and suggest compromises if necessary.

Participant Cue Card for Manager from the Philippines, a Japanese National, since no Local Filipino has yet been Found who seems Qualified to be Manager

You are a member of a conference which is to make recommendations to the Head Office (the President and Board of Directors) in Tokyo on the proposed changes in the corporate structure, and in the selection of an international language. Your particular concern is to ensure that the following are adequately incorporated into the suggestions for the corporation:

(1) *Dealing with the proposed reorganization:*
You like the plan. If you do a good job you can get back to the home office in Tokyo. You have been in the Philippines for two years and you are ready to go home. Your wife is homesick and your two children, aged five and seven, must now get a Japanese education or they will find it difficult to fit into Japanese society when they do return. Your friend is presently the vice president of the Eastern Division in Japan and he has said that if you do well as manager for one more year, he believes he can get you a place with his division.

(2) *Dealing with the selection of an international language:*

You are aware of the problem because you face it every day. Your position is that Japanese should be the language of Saito — not only the international language but also the in-country language. Presently Saito has the policy of using the local language whenever possible and this has created many problems for you in the Philippines. It would be much better if Japanese was the only language to be used. That is your suggestion.

In order to make certain that your points are properly dealt with by fellow delegates of the conference, it may be necessary to bring them up several times during the discussions. Be prepared to make and suggest compromises if needed.

Participant Cue Card for Manager from Singapore

You are a member of a conference which is to make recommendations to the Head Office (the President and Board of Directors) in Tokyo on the proposed changes in the corporate structure, and in the selection of an international language.

Your particular concern is to ensure that the following are adequately incorporated into the suggestions for the corporation:

(1) *Dealing with the proposed reorganization:*

You feel this is a very poor reorganizational plan. No flow chart should be so complicated. You think the present corporate plan, which was drawn up in 1970, is much better and should be kept. This new plan will create more problems that it solves.

(2) *Dealing with the selection of an international language:*

There is no question in your mind. The language has to be English. Singapore has four official languages: Malay, Tamil, Mandarin and English, and one national language, Malay. However, everyone knows that English is the international language of business. Saito should have made it the single international language from the beginning. You are pleased that it can do so now.

In order to make certain that your points are properly dealt with by fellow delegates of the conference, it may be necessary to bring them up several times during the discussions. Be prepared to make and suggest compromises if necessary.

Participant Cue Card for Manager from the Netherlands, who is a Japanese National, since no Local Dutch Manager has yet been Found

You are a member of a conference which is to make recommendations to the Head Office (the President and Board of Directors) in

Tokyo on the proposed changes in the corporate structure, and in the selection of an international language.

Your particular concern is to ensure that the following are adequately incorporated into the suggestions for the corporation:

(1) *Dealing with the proposed reorganization:*
This seems like a very poor plan to you. There are too many vice presidents and it is not clear if they are equal in power or not. It seems strange that although Japan is in Asia, there is a vice president for Japan and another vice president for Asia. You think it would be wiser if the leaders of the North American, South American, European and Asian divisions be called directors instead of vice presidents, and keep only two vice presidents, one for the entire international division and one for Japan.

(2) *Dealing with the selection of an international language:*
Your choice is French, Spanish, or English if it is necessary to have one single international language, but you would prefer a multilingual policy which allows for many languages to be used officially within the corporation.

In order to make certain that your points are properly dealt with by fellow delegates of the conference, it may be necessary to bring them up several times during the discussions. Be prepared to make and suggest compromises if necessary.

Participant Cue Card for Manager from France

You are a member of a conference which is to make recommendations to the Head Office (the President and Board of Directors) in Tokyo on the proposed changes in the corporate structure, and in the selection of an international language.

Your particular concern is to ensure that the following are adequately incorporated into the suggestions for the corporation:

(1) *Dealing with the proposed reorganization:*
You like it and you want to keep it exactly the way it is. You know you have a good chance of becoming the first vice president for Europe and you want to do a good job at this conference to impress these company managers, for you would like to become the vice president for International Affairs in the next few years.

(2) *Dealing with the selection of an international language:*
Your choice is French and you will suggest it, but not push for it. The selection of a language is not very important to you and you will go along with what you think is the majority view on this issue.

In order to make certain that your points are properly dealt with by fellow delegates of the conference, it may be necessary to bring them up several times during the discussions. Be prepared to make and suggest compromises if necessary.

Participant Cue Card for Manager from India

You are a member of a conference which is to make recommendations to the Head Office (the President and Board of Directors) in Tokyo on the proposed changes in the corporate structure, and in the selection of an international language.

Your particular concern is to ensure that the following are adequately incorporated into the suggestions for the corporation:

(1) *Dealing with the proposed reorganization:*
   The plan is OK but you feel it would be better to have Asia divided into different divisions, in order to encourage future expansion. You will suggest that the reorganization replaces Asia with South Asia, Southeast Asia, and East Asia, with vice presidents for each of them. This will more nearly parallel the North American and South American divisions. You also feel that Japan should be a part of the East Asia section and should not have a separate division with its own vice president.
(2) *Dealing with the selection of an international language:*
   Your choice is Hindi. It is an ancient language with a great literature. It is spoken by many millions of people in India and is studied as a foreign language by foreign students worldwide. The written script is difficult but will add prestige to the corporation.

In order to make certain that your points are properly dealt with by fellow delegates of the conference, it may be necessary to bring them up several times during the discussions. Be prepared to make and suggest compromises if necessary.

Participant Cue Card for Manager from the United States

You are a member of a conference which is to make recommendations to the Head Office (the President and Board of Directors) in Tokyo on the proposed changes in the corporate structure, and in the selection of an international language.

Your particular concern is to ensure that the following are adequately incorporated into the suggestions for the corporation:

(1) *Dealing with the proposed reorganization:*
   You completely agree with this proposal. In fact, you were on the committee which drew up these plans. As is clear from the

proposal, you will be the vice president for North America; and, since you expect Canada to join the corporation soon, you will automatically be in charge of all the offices in both these countries.

(2) *Dealing with the selection of an international language:*
You support the selection of English, because it is already the international language of business and, of the 14 countries which are members of Saito's international division, five of them use English in an official or semi-official way. Those countries are the United States, Great Britain, India, Singapore, and the Philippines. You feel English should not only be the international language of Saito but its *only* language.

In order to make certain that your points are properly dealt with by fellow delegates of the conference, it may be necessary to bring them up several times during the discussions. Be prepared to make and suggest compromises if necessary.

Participant Cue Card for Manager from Brazil

You are a member of a conference which is to make recommendations to the Head Office (the President and Board of Directors) in Tokyo on the proposed changes in the corporate structure, and in the selection of an international language.

Your particular concern is to ensure that the following are adequately incorporated into the suggestions for the corporation:

(1) *Dealing with the proposed reorganization:*
It looks very good to you, and you would like to keep it just the way it is. You do not want to be a part of the North American division and are very pleased that North America and South America have been kept separate.

(2) *Dealing with the selection of an international language:*
Your choice is Japanese, which is spoken widely in Brazil. You believe that since Saito is a Japanese company, all official business should be conducted in Japanese.

In order to make certain that your points are properly dealt with by fellow delegates of the conference, it may be necessary to bring them up several times during the discussions. Be prepared to make and suggest compromises if necessary.

Participant Cue Card for Manager from Great Britain

You are a member of a conference which is to make recommendations to the Head Office (the President and Board of Directors) in

Tokyo on the proposed changes in the corporate structure, and in the selection of an international language.

Your particular concern is to ensure that the following are adequately incorporated into the suggestions for the corporation:

(1) *Dealing with the proposed reorganization:*
    You do not like the idea of the French manager becoming vice president for Europe, and having to work under him, so you are opposed to the present proposed reorganization plan. Of course, you cannot say that directly, so you must think of other reasons why you do not approve of the present plan.

    Since the US and the UK divisions have always worked closely together and speak the same language, you suggest they form one division by themselves, perhaps called the 'English-speaking division'.

(2) *Dealing with the selection of an international language:*
    You feel there should be four languages of Saito rather than one, in order to correspond to the four divisions of the company. You propose an English division for the US and the UK (see above for reasons), a Spanish division for South America, a French division for Europe, and a Japanese division for Asia.

    You believe that if the company tries to limit itself to one international language now, it will result only in more confusion and hard feelings among the different divisions.

In order to make certain that your points are properly dealt with by fellow delegates of the conference, it may be necessary to bring them up several times during the discussions. Be prepared to make and suggest compromises if necessary.

Participant Cue Card for Manager from Taiwan

You are a member of a conference which is to make recommendations to the Head Office (the President and Board of Directors) in Tokyo on the proposed changes in the corporate structure, and in the selection of an international language.

Your particular concern is to ensure that the following are adequately incorporated into the suggestions for the corporation:

(1) *Dealing with the proposed reorganization:*
    You like it, except for one thing. You want to suggest the name of your country to be changed from Taiwan to China, so that when mainland China is opened to Saito, you will have a good chance to take over that very large division. Of course, you cannot tell the conference participants this, so you will say instead that there is only one China and that Taiwan is only a part of that China. Therefore, the name of the division should reflect the name of the country as other divisions do.

(2) *Dealing with the selection of an international language:*

You do not like the idea of choosing only one international language. You like the present policy of using the local language whenever possible and sending reports and all correspondence in the local language as well as Japanese.

If it is necessary to have fewer company languages, you will suggest that there be three: English for North America and Europe; Spanish for South America; and Standard Chinese (Mandarin) for Asia. Everything would continue to have a Japanese translation as well. In Asia, Mandarin is already used in Singapore and Taiwan, with many speakers of Mandarin in Hong Kong. Many Koreans and Japanese can read Chinese already, so that should not be a problem. If Standard Chinese is chosen, mainland China will be impressed, and it will be easier to establish a division there. That is important because of the cheap labour as well as the large potential market (population is one billion).

In order to make certain that your points are properly dealt with by fellow delegates of the conference, it may be necessary to bring them up several times during the discussions. Be prepared to make and suggest compromises if necessary.

Participant Cue Card for Manager from West Germany

You are a member of a conference which is to make recommendations to the Head Office (the President and Board of Directors) in Tokyo on the proposed changes in the corporate structure, and in the selection of an international language.

Your particular concern is to ensure that the following are adequately incorporated into the suggestions for the corporation:

(1) *Dealing with the proposed reorganization:*

It appears reasonable to you, but it is certainly clear that a single language must now be found as an international language for Saito, or the company will not be able to expand. There are already too many languages in use and this is the absolute limit of expansion until a single language is chosen.

(2) *Dealing with the selection of an international language:*

German is your choice, and you will nominate it, but you do not really expect it to be accepted. You will accept any language, but you do not want it to be English, since the Americans and the British seem so arrogant about speaking English.

In order to make sure your points are properly dealt with by fellow delegates of the conference, it may be necessary to bring them up several times during the discussion. Be prepared to make and suggest compromises if necessary.

Participant Cue Card for Manager from Italy

You are a member of a conference which is to make recommendations to the Head Office (the President and Board of Directors) in
Tokyo, on the proposed changes in the corporate structure and in
the selection of an international language.

No one at the conference knows this, and you do not plan to tell
anyone, but you have agreed to accept a job as president of an
Italian company within six months. Your new firm will not be in
competition with Saito, so you felt you could come to this meeting,
but you are reluctant to make any suggestions about either the
proposed changes or the selection of a language. You have worked
for Saito for five years and are glad to be leaving it, because there is
so much internal competition between the divisions.

'Teachers and Learners'

Objective: To illustrate how effective leaders use personality to
support knowledge and experience to motivate their followers.
Duration: From one-half to two hours, depending on size of group.
Number of players: From three to any number.
Materials: None.
Summary: The players, in pairs, take it in turns to teach something
to the group; then their strategies are discussed.

'Test with a Moral'

Objectives:
(1) To stimulate young players' critical abilities.
(2) To encourage them to be more active learners.
Duration: About 20 minutes.
Number of players: Any number.
Summary: Players are asked to complete a questionnaire which has
a 'sting in the tail'.

'Them and Us'

Objectives: To study the effects of ascribed status and power — and
the lack of them — on powerful and powerless members of society.
Duration: About an hour and a half.
Number of players: At least ten.
Materials:
(1) The full setting for a coffee break, as described in the game.

(2) Role instructions, as described in the game.
Summary: When players break for coffee they find themselves in a discriminatory situation where one group is more privileged than the other. After the break they discuss their experiences.

'Think of a Cube'

Objectives:
(1) To stretch players' imagination.
(2) To explore differences in people's visual, auditory and feelings-oriented responses to situations.
Duration: About half an hour.
Number of players: Any number.
Summary: An exercise in imagination.

'Thumbs Up'

Objective: To draw attention to the different ways people perceive and therefore solve problems.
Duration: From ten minutes to about an hour.
Number of players: Three or more.
Materials: None.
Summary: Individuals are asked to fold and refold their hands and arms; then to give feedback to their neighbours about their feelings, which is posted for general discussion.

'To Be Or Not...'

Objective: To promote understanding of the differences between individual and team behaviour.
Duration: About 20 minutes.
Number of players: Any number over six.
Materials: None
Summary: Players learn to form 'group sentences' from individual words.

'Walk-On'

Objective: To study self-presentation.
Duration: At least an hour.
Number of players: Minimum of three.

Materials: A complete video recording system (video recorder with camera, monitor and playback).
Summary: The players, in small groups, are videotaped in discussion; then the tape is replayed for feedback on their verbal and non-verbal communication styles.

'What Would You Do If...'

Objective: To provide practice in cross-cultural negotiation.
Duration: About an hour.
Number of players: At least four.
Materials: Role instructions as described in the game.
Summary: The game consists of several dialogues between people from different cultures. In each situation a misunderstanding has arisen which the role-makers try to sort out.

'Who's the Leader?'

Objective: To study possible connections between leadership effectiveness and the personal presentation of the leader.
Duration: About an hour.
Number of players: Any number over five.
Materials: Dressing-up clothes, jewellery, hats, buttons, badges, etc.
Summary: Players use costumes and 'props' to dress up according to their perceptions of 'a leader'; then discuss the effects they create.

'You Choose'

Objectives:
(1) To develop group behaviour.
(2) To generate creative thinking.
(3) To study leadership behaviour.
(4) To study group motivation.
Duration: One to two and a half hours, depending on numbers.
Number of players: from five to any number of people who can be accommodated in one room.
Materials: None.
Summary: Players in sub-groups have to invent a game for the whole group to play; then report on the process to the class, including rating their leader.

Bibliography

Belbin, R Meredith (1981) *Management Teams: Why They Succeed or Fail*. London: Heinemann.

Bergson, Henri (1956) 'Laughter' *in* Wylie Sypher *The Meaning of Comedy*. New York: Doubleday.

Berne, Eric (1964) *Games People Play*. New York: Grove Press.

Burns Elizabeth (1972) *Theatricality: A Study of Convention in the Theatre and in Social Life*. London: Longman.

Cameron, Kim S and David A Whetton (1983) 'A Model for Teaching Management Skills' *from* Whetton, D A and Cameron, K S (1984) *Developing Management Skills*. Glenview, Illinois: Scott, Foresman and Co.

Campbell, Donald T and Julian C Stanley (1963) *Experimental and Quasi-Experimental Designs for Research*. Chicago: Rand McNally.

Dewey, John (1974) *John Dewey on Education: Selected Writings*, Chicago: University of Chicago Press.

Duke, Richard (1975) *Gaming: the Future's Language*. Beverly Hills: Sage Publications.

Elgood, Chris (1981) *Handbook of Management Games*. UK: Gower Publishing Co.

Fiedler, Fred F and Martin M Chemers (1974) *Leadership and Effective Management*. Glenview, Illinois: Scott, Foresman and Co.

Goffman, Irving (1975) *The Presentation of Self in Everyday Life*. New Jersey: Prentice-Hall.

Guthrie, Sir Tyrone (1971) *Tyrone Guthrie on Acting*, London: Studio Vista.

Hersey, Paul (1984) *The Situational Leader*. Center for Leadership Studies.

Hersey, Paul and Kenneth H Blanchard (1977) *Management of Organizational Behavior: Utilizing Human Resources*, 3rd edition. New York: Prentice-Hall.

Hope, Joanne (1986) *Games Nurses Play*. Sydney: Pergamon.

Knowles, Malcolm S (1970) *The Modern Practice of Adult Education: Andragogy versus Pedagogy*, New York: Association Press.

Kolb, David A, Irwin M Rubin and James M MacIntyre (1984) *Organizational Psychology: an Experiential Approach to Organizational Behavior*. New Jersey: Prentice Hall.

Laver, Michael (1979) *Playing Politics*. UK, Harmondsworth, Middlesex: Penguin Books.

Lineham, Thomas E and Barbara Ellis Long (1970) *The Road Game*. New York: Herder and Herder.

Livingston, S and C S Stoll (1973) *Simulation Games: an Introduction for the Social Studies Teacher*. New York: Free Press.

Moore, Barry (1978) *Australian Management Games*. Sydney, Australia: University of New South Wales Press.

Moore, Peter (1987) *Let's Have Moore Drama*. Sydney: Methuen.

Parsons, Talcott (1962) 'The School Class as a Social System', *in* A H Halsey, J Floud and C A Anderson (eds) *Education, Economy and Society*. New York: Glencoe Free Press.

Pfeiffer, J, William and John E Jones (1975) *A Handbook of Structured Experiences for Human Relations Training*. La Jolla, California: University Associates.

Reddin, W J (1971) *Effective Management by Objectives: the 3-D Method of MBO*. New York: McGraw Hill.

Rogers, Carl R (1969) *Freedom to Learn*. Columbus, Ohio: Merrill.

Stanislavsky, Constantin (1962) *An Actor Prepares* (translated by ERH). London: Geoffrey Bles. First published 1937.

Stone, Elizabeth (1981) 'A Game for APACE' *in APACE*, No 13, December 1981. PO Box 81, Wentworth Building, Sydney University, Australia 2006.

Via, Richard A and Larry E Smith (1983) *Talk and Listen: English as an International Language via Drama Techniques*. Oxford: Pergamon.

Walford, Rex (1979) *Simulation Games in the Classroom*. London: Longford.

Index